T0351359

American Presidents and Oliver Stone

American Presidents and Oliver Stone

Kennedy, Nixon, and Bush between History and Cinema

Carl Freedman

Bristol, UK / Chicago, USA

First published in the UK in 2020 by
Intellect, The Mill, Parnall Road, Fishponds, Bristol, BS16 3JG, UK

First published in the USA in 2020 by
Intellect, The University of Chicago Press, 1427 E. 60th Street,
Chicago, IL 60637, USA

A catalogue record for this book is available from
the British Library.

Copy editor: MPS Technologies
Cover designer: Aleksandra Szumlas
Production manager: Emma Berrill
Typesetting: Newgen

Print ISBN 978-1-78938-262-4
ePDF ISBN 978-1-78938-263-1
ePUB ISBN 978-1-78938-264-8

Printed and bound by Hobbs, UK

To find out about all our publications, please visit
www.intellectbooks.com.
There, you can subscribe to our e-newsletter,
browse or download our current catalogue,
and buy any titles that are in print.

This is a peer-reviewed publication.

An die Nachgeborenen—

Brandon, Finnegan, Leila, Martin, Rachel, Rosa, Simon, and Stephen—

And, as always and forever,

To Annette—

And to the memory of my father, Leon Freedman (1921–2013), with whom, had it been possible, I would have discussed every page

". . .and yet I often think it odd that it [history] should be so dull, for a great deal of it must be invention."

—Catherine Morland in Jane Austen's *Northanger Abbey*

Contents

Introduction

This volume attempts to construct a critical genre through the synthesis of two genres in which I have worked in the past: historical and political analysis, on the one hand, and, on the other, film studies. My aim is to transcend the limitations of both formalism and empiricism while, at the same time, making use of the genuine insights that both approaches have to offer. Before briefly outlining the theoretical infrastructure of this project, I will say a few words about the artist whose work provides the project's occasion.

No current filmmaker—probably no filmmaker of any era—has displayed a greater interest in American history than Oliver Stone. To be sure, not all his movies are historically oriented. For example, *U-Turn* (1997), a savage, darkly comedic, and much underrated neo-noir crime thriller, is set in an only vaguely contemporary present rather than at any particularly exact time. Then too, *Natural Born Killers* (1994) and *Any Given Sunday* (1999) are historical only in a fairly general way, as they examine the corruptions of the mass media and of big-time professional sports, respectively, during the final decade of the twentieth century. But most of Stone's best and most acclaimed films take very specific historical events and personalities for their raw material—and usually events involving Stone's own country.[1] *Salvador* (1986), Stone's first important film (as a director), engages US involvement in El Salvador during the period of civil war, assassinations, and right-wing death squads. His trilogy of films about the Vietnam War—*Platoon* (1986), *Born on the Fourth of July* (1989), and *Heaven & Earth* (1993)—is rivaled, perhaps, only by Francis Ford Coppola's *Apocalypse Now* (1979) as providing the closest we have to a definitive cinematic treatment of the first war that America lost. His two films about Wall Street—*Wall Street* (1987) and *Wall Street: Money Never Sleeps* (2010)—perform the uncommon feat of finding human drama among the stratospheric machinations of US-based finance capital.[2]

In the following pages, I will examine three of Stone's other historical films, namely, those that focus on the individual person-alities of three US presidents: *JFK* (1991), *Nixon* (1995), and *W.* (2008). *JFK* and *Nixon* are Stone's longest and most ambitious films, and between them, in their high seriousness, offer a gener-ally (though not totally) pessimistic account of America from the 1960s to the early 1970s. *W.*, which deals with the first decade of the new century, is much slighter and considerably lighter in tone, forming a gloomily comic—indeed, almost grotesque—sequel to the earlier downbeat duology.

It is worth noting that, in addition to the fiction films mentioned above, Stone has also expressed his interest in history through a number of nonfictional documentaries. The most important of these is the twelve-part television series, *The Untold History of the United States* (2012–2013), which ought to be considered along with the exactly contemporary book of the same title—a lengthy and heavily footnoted volume that Stone co-authored with the profes-sional historian Peter Kuznick. Hyperbole is a figure that Stone not infrequently uses, and the title of the book and the series is indeed somewhat hyperbolic. Neither the series nor the volume covers the whole history of the country; the subject is rather the United States during the twentieth and early twenty-first centuries, with particular emphasis on foreign and military policy. Nor do Stone and Kuznick relate a genuinely "untold" story. On the contrary, what they offer is mainly a vast and skillful summary of work by many well-known historians and journalists: primarily, scholars of what was once called the "revisionist" school, but who are more usefully described simply as students of history who write about the United States in the commonsense way that powerful nations other than the United States are nearly always written about—that is, as a country that has normally used its power to promote and defend, largely through violence and fraud, what the dominant forces of the country have perceived to be the nation's socio-economic and political interests. The story is "untold" only in the sense that it varies from the more-or-less "official" story typically promulgated by most politicians and enshrined in school textbooks. Intrinsically useful for the student, especially the beginning student, of American history, the series and the book are useful for the viewer of Stone's films in providing a capacious account of Stone's view of his country's past, one written in the cold prose of historiography, so to speak, rather than in the "poetry" of cinema.

There are two antithetical ways that Stone's historical films have often been considered—both of which this book rejects. On the one hand, many commentators—especially historians and journalists with no particular knowledge of or interest in film as an art form—have frequently approached Stone's fiction films as though they were nonfictional works of history, and have attempted to evaluate them for factual accuracy. Sometimes such evaluations have been laudatory. For instance, many of those familiar with the day-to-day inner workings of financial trading have praised *Wall Street* for its sure knowledge of the details of Wall Street life, even when they have sometimes objected to the basically condemnatory attitude that the film takes to the lifeworld it depicts. Likewise, many of Stone's fellow Vietnam combat veterans have been impressed by the "realism" of *Platoon*. More often, though, the attitude of those who have tried to "grade" Stone's films as though they were term papers submitted by a pupil in a history class has been harsh.

The most extreme example here is *JFK*, which, as we shall see, was subjected, upon its release—and, indeed, even *before* its release— to a campaign of vituperation unequalled by the reception of any other movie in Hollywood history. Of the huge number of attacks claiming that Stone had gotten the facts of the Kennedy assassination wrong, virtually none paid even the slightest attention to the plain fact that *JFK* is a work of cinematic art.

The opposite of this crudely fact-oriented response to Stone's films is to take refuge in Alfred Hitchcock's famous maxim, "It's only a movie"—an approach that, though never adopted by Stone himself, has sometimes served as a defense mounted by others against objections to the films' supposed failures of accuracy. This approach stresses that a movie is not a work of historical scholarship, and is therefore not to be judged by the same standards. *JFK* is a tautly constructed thriller, brilliantly acted and filmed at a virtually unsurpassed level of technical sophistication—*that*, it has been argued, is how it ought be judged, rather than on the basis of whether or not it succeeds in solving the many real-life mysteries of Dealey Plaza.

The formalism of this approach has the advantage of treating cinema *as* cinema rather than as something else, and of directing our attention to the aesthetic richness and complexity of Stone's work. At the same time, and like all formalism, it runs the risk of trivializing the objects of its consideration. The intentionality of *JFK* and *Nixon* and *W.*—which is not quite the same thing as the subjective intentions of Oliver Stone as an individual, though it is certainly not unrelated to them—is inseparable from the actual personalities, events, patterns, and issues of modern US history. Though it is certainly possible to enjoy these films simply as entertainments and to subject them to a merely immanent formal criticism, to do so is to ignore a great deal of what they have to offer. For all its aesthetic and epistemological *naïveté*, the vulgar historicism that would judge Stone's work according to a crudely empirical standard does at least grasp that his movies invite us to grapple with issues different from and in the long run vastly weightier than casting and camera angles.

Stone, of course, is by no means the first artist to mine the history of his country for raw material that is transmuted into works of fiction. Tolstoy and Sir Walter Scott are among his more illustrious predecessors in this regard, but the most illustrious of them all—and, I believe, the one who has had the greatest influence on Stone himself—is surely Shakespeare. Nearly a third of the plays in the Shakespeare *oeuvre* are those generally designated histories, and, as Jan Kott has pointed out more convincingly, perhaps, than any other critic,[3] the essentially political concerns of the histories animate many of the tragedies as well. Like Stone, Shakespeare has sometimes been judged on the empirical accuracy of his work and found wanting. Consider *Richard III*, one of the most popular of the histories and the earliest Shakespeare play still widely performed and read (in the modern era, the titular role has been played by Laurence Olivier, Alec Guinness, Ian McKellan, Kenneth Branagh, Mark Rylance, and many other major actors). There is actually an entire organization (the Richard III Society, whose website may be found at http://www.richardiii.net/index.php) that is largely devoted to arguing that Richard of Gloucester was really quite a good monarch, and not at all the monstrously evil Machiavellian schemer portrayed by Shakespeare.

Yet, even if all the claims of Richard's admirers were assumed, for the sake of argument, to be valid, no rational Shakespeare critic could suppose that that disposes of the interest of the play. "Shakespeare," as T. S. Eliot wrote, "acquired more *essential* history from Plutarch [and, he might have added, from Holinshed, Shakespeare's chief source for English and Scottish history] than most men could from the whole British Museum" (emphasis added).[4] The proof of Eliot's assertion is to be found in the plays themselves. We know that Shakespeare acquired a vast amount of "essential" history because the plays convey a vast amount. Though Eliot does not explicitly define what he means by essential history, the point seems to derive from Eliot's favorite philosopher. In the famous ninth chapter of the *Poetics*, Aristotle proclaims poetry (in the sense of all imaginative or fictional discourse) to be more *philosophical* than history (by which Aristotle evidently means the merely factual chronicle): "The true difference is that one [history] relates what has happened, the other [poetry] what may happen."[5] For our purposes, we may understand essential history to mean the most fundamental and general patterns of the historical process—those that determine "what may happen," as Aristotle says—as they are manifest in a particular time and place but also, possibly, in others. Great work does not "transcend" its historical moment (in the sense of leaving it behind) but penetrates so deeply into it as to be of enduring interest and value. The discrete facts of the chronicler or the empiricist are not, of course, wholly irrelevant to essential history, but neither can the latter be reduced to the factually accurate chronicle or judged by its standards. *Richard III* is a penetrating study of fifteenth-century English political history—and, by extension, of much other history too—regardless of the play's strict factual reliability. Nothing that the enthusiasts of the Richard III Society say can degrade the value of *Richard III*: just as nothing proposed by the admirers of the Warren Report or the enemies of Jim Garrison can nullify the interest of *JFK*.

Stone's importance as an artist is, obviously, not equal to Shakespeare's. But sometimes smaller things can profitably be compared to greater ones. Films like *JFK*, *Nixon*, and *W.* are comparable to plays like *Richard III*, *Richard II*, *Henry V*, *Julius Caesar*, and *Macbeth* in the sense that they are all works of art that use aesthetic techniques to consider problems of history and, more specifically, problems of leadership and governance. No sane viewer or reader would approach Shakespeare as a historian rather than as a poet and playwright. But it is only by appreciating him as a poet and playwright that we can see how his work offers an understanding of what Eliot called "essential history" that is more wide-ranging and profound than that of perhaps any other writer whom we know, professional historians included. Likewise, we need to approach Stone as a filmmaker—indeed, as a dramatist, as he has more than once described himself—in order to grasp how and to what degree his films can illuminate issues of modern American history (and perhaps of other history too). The matter may be put like this. When *Richard III* first appeared on the stage, the civil wars of fifteenth-century England were a fresh, and deeply disturbing, historical memory for the viewers. Yet the play retains its vitality for many who have no special interest in or knowledge of the time and place that the play dramatizes. We do not yet know whether *Nixon* (a drama about another evil political Richard)[6] will continue to seem exciting for audiences that need to be told who Kissinger and H. R. Haldeman and even Nixon himself were. But the gamble of this book is that it will—that, indeed, all of the three films considered will live beyond their historical moment, not by attempting to *transcend* it (any more than Shakespeare's histories attempt to transcend fourteenth- and fifteenth-century England) but by capturing some fundamental insights about modern America, and perhaps much else. In the pages that follow, I will indeed have a good deal to say about Kennedy and Nixon and Bush as known to (nonfictional—which is not to say univocal) history as well as to Stone's historical fictions: not in order to "grade" the latter against the former, but rather better to understand just what kind of insight Stone's movies provide. The sunny hopefulness of Kennedy, the tormented evil of Nixon, and the pathetic silliness of Bush were not invented by Oliver Stone: but neither do his representations of these matters have any claim to being exhaustive or unproblematic. They do, however, have a claim to teach us a good deal, and not only about three individual personalities. This volume will attempt to demonstrate how. It is in this way that my general method is to combine—and, I hope, successfully to synthesize—film criticism with historico-political analysis, with the goal of giving new strength and life to both.

I should add one thing. I have never before written about George W. Bush at all, and I have never written about John Kennedy at great length. But I have written an entire book about Richard Nixon, a book, in fact, that contains some brief commentary on *Nixon* and *JFK*.[7] Since I dislike repeating myself, I have tried to reduce overlap between that book and this one to the barest essential minimum; but, since I cannot assume that all readers of this book will be familiar with the earlier one, some repetition has proved inevitable. I ask those who *have* read the earlier book to bear with it.

It remains to express my gratitude to those who have helped to give this book whatever merit it possesses—with, of course, the normal understanding that none of them is in any way responsible for any flaws and shortcomings that may remain, which are exclusively my own responsibility. As ever, I am indebted to more people than I can name; but I will do my best to particularize the most important debts of which I am aware. I mention the following individuals according to alphabetical order by surname. Stacia Haynie, the provost of my university, appointed me to my current professorship, one whose reduced teaching duties freed up some of the time in which the book was composed. Christopher Kendrick, my closest co-thinker since our long-ago days in graduate school together, read the entire book in manuscript and contributed many characteristically acute suggestions. Joseph Kronick, the chair of my department, awarded me a research grant that was important in helping with the late stages of the book's composition. Daniel Lindvall, the editor of *Film International*, has robustly supported my work in film criticism for many years, most recently by publishing an earlier version of the Kennedy chapter of this book. Stephen Peltier, in a precise instance of "without whom this book would never have been written," suggested to me the basic idea for it in the first place. Grover Proctor generously shared with me his wide-ranging scholarly knowledge of the Kennedy assassination. Steven Shaviro, whose profound understanding of both cinema and American political history (among other matters) has been an assistance and an inspiration to me for decades, was once again unfailingly helpful. Jelena Stanovnik, my editor at Intellect, provided—not for the first time—indispensable support and guidance in turning a manuscript of mine into a book. Finally, I must mention, though I cannot name, the two anonymous peer-reviewers for Intellect, who provided encouragement and valuable suggestions for revision; both were exemplary in understanding what I was trying to do and in helping me to do it better.

My greatest debt by far is, as always, to my wife, Annette Peltier Freedman. She read the book in manuscript, discussed it very usefully with me, and, in addition, made life, for me, much better worth living in every other way as well.

CHAPTER I
Kennedy: Icon

Kennedy: Icon

To Assassinate a Movie

In December 1991, Oliver Stone released *JFK*, a more than three-hour film that focuses on, and fictionalizes, the investigation that Jim Garrison, the District Attorney of Orleans Parish, Louisiana, conducted into the murder of President John F. Kennedy.[8] It was, in the standard Hollywood parlance, a "major motion picture." Stone's earlier films had established him as one of Hollywood's most successful directors: a winner of multiple Oscars and Golden Globes, who worked with major studios and commanded big budgets and popular stars. He was (and is) known both for extraordinary technical virtuosity and, as we have seen, for his passionate interest in modern American history, especially the Vietnam War (of which he is a decorated combat veteran). *JFK* was made at Warner Brothers on a budget of roughly $40,000,000. In the leading role of Jim Garrison, it stars Kevin Costner, then at the very peak of his career. Costner had recently directed, co-produced, and starred in *Dances with Wolves* (1990), winning Oscars for Best Picture and Best Director and receiving an Oscar nomination for Best Actor. Few, if any, of Hollywood's leading men were at that time more popular and respected. *JFK* co-stars, as Garrison's wife Liz, Sissy Spacek, herself an Oscar winner and frequent Oscar nominee. The film is also notable for featuring numerous major film and television stars, most in relatively small roles: Ed Asner, Kevin Bacon, John Candy, Tommy Lee Jones, Jack Lemmon, Walter Matthau, Laurie Metcalf (at that time very popular for her supporting role in the television sitcom *Roseanne* [ABC, 1988–1997]), Gary Oldman, Joe Pesci, and Donald Sutherland, among others.

It is unsurprising that, with so much talent and so many resources behind it, *JFK* was received very favorably by the nation's film reviewers, and went on to win various awards (including Oscars for Best Cinematography and Best Film Editing, and a Golden Globes award for Stone as Best Director) and to gross, worldwide, more than five times its budget. But the reaction of America's political journalists was very different from that of film critics and the filmgoing public. Beginning even *before* the movie's release (mainly on the basis of purloined early versions of the screenplay), dozens of prominent (and not-so-prominent) journalists—most of whom had never displayed any particular knowledge of or interest in either cinema or the Kennedy assassination—launched a campaign of condemnation against Stone's film that remains unparalleled in American history. Across the political spectrum, conservatives and liberals alike formed a chorus of denunciation, generally maintaining that the treatment of history in *JFK* was not simply inadequate or erroneous but somehow evil and shameful. Never, before or since, have the prime keepers of the nation's everyday political discourse seemed so determined to destroy a movie—in many cases, even before the public had had a chance to watch it. Sometimes the attackers even derogated the film's artistic quality, nearly always without any supporting argument.

To document the particulars of the campaign against *JFK* in even a remotely thorough way would require far more space than the effort would be worth for our purposes. But a few examples will be useful in giving some taste of the extraordinary obloquy that the film met. The attack by Tom Wicker of *The New York Times*—at that time one of America's leading liberal journalists and the author of two popular books about Kennedy—was fairly typical. Wicker's contribution—a cover story in his newspaper's entertainment section—was the most prominent of the roughly thirty separate items that the *Times* (which likes to style itself as America's "paper of record") printed in its attack on Stone's movie. Wicker titled his article, "Does *JFK* Conspire Against Reason?", and maintained not only that "Mr. Stone insists on one true faith about November 22, 1963," but, furthermore, that "he uses the powerful instrument of a motion picture, and relies on stars of the entertainment world, to propagate the one true faith—even though that faith, if widely accepted, would be contemptuous of the very Constitutional government Mr. Stone's film purports to uphold."[9] Since the film, as Wicker would have known had he watched it with even minimally serious attention, does not commit itself to any specific or detailed theory of the assassination, it is hard to know what is meant by the "one true faith": still less how that faith (as expressed, perhaps, in Garrison's deeply patriotic summation to the jury?) could threaten constitutional government. The *bad* faith with which Wicker himself approached the whole matter is illustrated by his statement that the film had caused controversy the summer before it was released when a draft of the screenplay "found its way to the press" (242). The draft script, obviously, did not "find its way" anywhere. It was *stolen*, evidently by a person or persons determined to discredit a movie that no member of the filmgoing public could yet have seen.

In 1991, George Will of *The Washington Post* occupied an eminence among conservative journalists more-or-less comparable to Wicker's among liberal ones. On the matter of *JFK*, they were pretty much in agreement: save that Will, in a column called, "*JFK*: Paranoid History," relied more heavily than Wicker on personal insults, and that, whereas Wicker appeared not to have watched the film with any care, Will appeared not to have watched it at all. Will claimed that the film portrays "a conspiracy of many thousands," something not suggested even as a remote possibility in *JFK*. "In his three-hour lie," Will wrote, "Stone falsifies so much that he may be an intellectual sociopath, indifferent to truth"—without documenting a single supposed "falsification," or explaining exactly how a fiction film "falsifies" in the first place. While ignoring the film Stone actually made, Will claimed to be able to diagnose the director's psychological condition: "He is a specimen of 1960s arrested development." This seems an especially weird claim, since, as he has often made clear, Stone, in the 1960s, was, like Will himself, a political conservative.[10] Will concluded his review by describing the film he evidently did not see as "an act of execrable history and contemptible citizenship by a man of technical skill, scant education and negligible conscience."[11] Compared to Will's column, Wicker's piece almost looks like a model of integrity.

Though he was never precisely a journalist, it is worthwhile to consider Jack Valenti's contribution to the onslaught against *JFK*. What was remarkable here is that Valenti, after serving for several years as a close and somewhat buffoonish aide to Lyndon Johnson, became, for nearly four decades, the president of the Motion Picture Association of America, the Hollywood trade organization. As such, his job was to do everything he could to promote Hollywood movies. To *attack* the films made by his employers—and especially a film produced by so economically important a studio as Warner Brothers—was the exact opposite of what was expected of him. Nonetheless, the year after *JFK*'s release, Valenti issued a strangely incoherent and emotional statement whose main point was to compare (or perhaps almost to equate) Stone's film with *Triumph of the Will* (1935), Leni Riefenstahl's famous (or infamous) pro-Nazi documentary about the Nazi Party's 1934 rally in Nuremberg. Exactly what the two films supposedly had in common was left totally unclear; but Valenti presumably thought that to insinuate any kind of similarity between Stone and a Nazi filmmaker was the most effective conceivable insult. In an especially bizarre touch, Valenti suggested that each film should have carried a disclaimer stating that "its contents were mostly pure fiction."[12] *JFK* of course *is* a work of fiction, and clearly presented as such. But *Triumph of the Will* is not fictional at all. It is a purely nonfictional documentary, which records an actual historical event without actors or a single frame of scripted footage. When Hollywood's number-one lobbyist hopelessly confuses elementary categories of filmmaking—while also, as it happened, misstating the date of Riefenstahl's film by six years—it seems clear that anything was acceptable if its aim was to destroy Stone's movie.

Finally, we may examine the response to *JFK* of a journalist— but not a political journalist—who *praised* the film: Roger Ebert of *The Chicago Sun-Times*, America's most influential journalistic film critic. In Ebert's review published just after the film's release, he applauded the film's aesthetic brilliance, calling it "a master-piece of film assembly" and predicting, "Film students will examine this film in wonder in the years to come." Ebert also devoted a good deal of space to expressing sympathy with the notion that Kennedy was murdered by a conspiracy. Though he declined—like the film itself—to propound any single theory of conspiracy, Ebert maintained that he had been reading books and articles about the assassination for a quarter century and had yet to find a convincing defense of the notion that Kennedy was murdered by a single shooter. He stated flatly that the physical evidence alone excluded that possibility: "One man with one rifle could not physically have caused what happened on Nov. 22, 1963, in Dallas."[13] Ebert would live to regret these words.

For more than a decade later, Ebert published another response to *JFK*, this one in his series of essays called "Great Movies." As the rubric suggests, Ebert continued to find the film aesthetically superb, again describing it as a masterpiece. Yet he also—without *quite* renouncing his earlier view that the assassination was the work of a conspiracy—had far less to say on the whole matter of conspiracy; and what he did say was much weaker and more qualified. Now the idea that one rifleman fired all the shots that rang out over Dealey Plaza was not said to be sheerly impossible, as Ebert had originally proclaimed it to be, but merely something that contradicts "our gut feelings" and "our dark suspicions." In the second paragraph of his article, Ebert provided a clue to his change of tune. He described a verbal attack upon himself by the most prestigious figure (at that time) in American broadcast journalism, probably in American journalism as a whole: "Shortly after the film was released, I ran into Walter Cronkite, and received a tongue-lashing, aimed at myself and my colleagues who had praised *JFK*. There was not, he said, a shred of truth in it." Ebert went on to paraphrase several further unargued insults by Cronkite, and then, astonishingly, conceded, "I have no doubt Cronkite was correct, from his point of view." Evidently terrorized into submission, Ebert defended himself only to the extent of limply pleading that, as a film critic, he was concerned with feelings rather than, like Cronkite, with facts.[14] That the journalistic campaign against *JFK* could intimidate someone of Ebert's stature and usual independence of mind is a telling indication of just how savage and unremitting it was.

What was the real point behind all the relentless attacks? The most obvious answer is simply that Stone's film sets itself against the report of the President's Commission on the Assassination of President Kennedy, more generally known as the Warren Report after Chief Justice Earl Warren, the chairman of the commission that President Johnson appointed to investigate his predecessor's murder. Though not all of the journalists who attacked Stone professed complete fealty to the Warren Report, it is generally true that to question its basic finding—that Kennedy was shot to death by a single individual named Lee Oswald,[15] acting alone for reasons best known to himself—has never been acceptable to the gatekeepers of the mainstream media. Indeed, so sacrosanct has the "lone gunman" theory of the Kennedy assassination been ever since the release of the Warren Report in September 1964, that, in order to discredit the alternative notion that the assassination was the work of a conspiracy (that is, of two or more people acting together), hegemonic journalistic discourse has virtually insinuated the nonexistence of conspiracies *tout court*: not only in the context of the Kennedy assassination but in almost any context at all. The term "conspiracy theorist" has been generally constructed to connote not just error but monomania and near-insanity: so that to suggest the possibility of conspiracy is *ipso facto* to announce oneself as a delusional paranoiac. The negative contention that conspiracies never take place—unprovable and wildly implausible though it be—has become a tacit assumption of respectable political discourse.

Stone's offense, moreover, was to suggest conspiracy not in a long, dry, heavily detailed factual book of the sort that comparatively few Americans would ever read—as many critics of the Warren Report had done—but, precisely, in a "major motion picture": a film featuring enormously popular stars and superstars and one that moviegoers tended to find irresistibly watchable, with hardly a single dull moment throughout its considerable length. In the 27 years that the Warren Report had stood before the world prior to the release of *JFK*, it had never found so popular and effective an opponent as Stone. The hysteria of the campaign to destroy *JFK* was in large part a response to the latter's evident effectiveness.

Of course, Stone was far from the first person to question the lone-gunman theory. Though it is no part of my purpose here to say what really happened in Dallas on November 22, 1963, it is worth bearing in mind that, while the Warren Report has always gone almost unquestioned in mainstream political journalism, most (though not quite all) of those who have examined it seriously and in detail have found it to be, at the very least, unsatisfactory. Many independent investigators have offered research to discredit the Warren Report.[16] But perhaps the most important example here is the most thorough official investigation into the murder of President Kennedy, namely that conducted between 1976 and 1978 by the United States House of Representatives Select Committee on Assassinations (HSCA). Though the HSCA did not question the good faith of the members of the Warren Commission, they did find fault with the Commission's competence; and they rejected the central finding of the Warren Report, the lone-gunman theory. The HSCA found a high probability that there had been a conspiracy to murder Kennedy, with at least two gunmen involved in the actual shooting. The Committee did not specify the precise nature of the conspiracy, and recommended further investigation into the matter by the Department of Justice. This recommendation has never been implemented. But Stone's *JFK* inspired enormous public interest in the unanswered questions surrounding the assassination; and in 1992, mainly in response to this public interest, Congress did create the Assassination Records Review Board to collect and make publicly available a good many primary documents relating to the assassination that had previously been kept under seal. Thanks to Stone's movie, millions of pages of documents pertinent to the assassination saw the light of day.[17]

If, then, the crime of *JFK* in the eyes of the nation's journalistic establishment was to reject the Warren Report and to suggest a conspiracy to assassinate Kennedy, the further question must be *why* the film's particular opposition to the Warren Report was such an ideological crime—even though the plausibility of the Report had long been undermined, and not only by individual "conspiracy theorists," but by an agency of the US government itself in an investigation far more extensive, patient, and careful than the Warren Commission's own. In this chapter I will propose an answer to this question. To do so, however, it is necessary to analyze the film at some length—and, before doing that, to consider the political significance of the person at the center of the whole controversy.

As the title of Stone's film indicates, that person is President John Fitzgerald Kennedy.

JFK: American Melbourne

More than half a century after his death, John Kennedy remains a stunningly familiar figure to Americans (and not only Americans) with even the slightest historical sense. His career has been documented, discussed, and dramatized so often, and in so many different ways, that it may be useful to approach him from an unusual angle: namely, through the text that he often named as his favorite book, Lord David Cecil's *The Young Melbourne* (1939). It was quite an unconventional choice. American politicians, when asked to identify a favorite literary work, generally either play it completely safe and name the Bible, or else choose some other widely revered book that is meant to imply the public virtues with which they hope to be identified. Ronald Reagan said that he particularly enjoyed reading *The Federalist Papers* (1788); and, especially after Kennedy's assassination, his own *Profiles in Courage* (1956) became a popular choice for Democrats. Kennedy's favorite, by contrast, is a somewhat racy biography of an English aristocrat and politician little known in America—and even in England remembered mainly as the aging political mentor to the young Queen Victoria—written by another English aristocrat, an academic literary critic and distant relative of his subject.

Why did JFK choose it as his favorite? The book is not without its intrinsic merits. Combining scholarly and impressionistic approaches, Cecil displays some of the talents of the novelists he studied in producing a vivid and entertaining portrait of William Lamb, 2nd Viscount Melbourne (1779–1848). The narrative moves effortlessly between Melbourne's public and private lives (the volume's full title is, *The Young Melbourne: And the Story of His Marriage with Caroline Lamb*), and conveys a sense not only of

Melbourne himself but of the time and place in which he flourished. Cecil presents Melbourne as one of the last flowers—and certainly not the least one—of the landed Whig aristocracy that was rooted in the eighteenth century but that, perhaps most notably in Melbourne's own person, survived into the Victorian age. Exquisitely written, *The Young Melbourne* is almost irresistibly readable.

But there was much more than that in the book for JFK to like. A thumbnail description of the young Melbourne can double as one of the young Kennedy: rich, handsome, intelligent, charming, born to great privilege, self-confident, devoted to his family, attractive to men and doubly attractive to women—and mightily attracted *by* beautiful women as well. There must have been many points at which JFK, as he read through Cecil's volume, almost felt as though he were looking into a mirror. Here, for instance, is Cecil's description of Lamb and his fellow Whig nobles: "They had that effortless knowledge of the world that comes only to those, who from childhood have been accustomed to move in a complex society; that delightful unassertive confidence possible only to people who have never had cause to doubt their social position."[18] This was John Kennedy to a tee. Though his father, Joseph Kennedy Sr., never quite got over the way that the Protestant Brahmins of Boston looked down on the Irish Catholic newcomers, however accomplished, the son was beyond such resentments. Raised in a wealthy and politically well-connected household, educated at Choate and at Harvard, and familiar with the high society of Boston, New York, and London, JFK never had cause to feel insecure of his social position in any company whatever. Or consider Cecil's account of the Lamb family: "By the time they were grown up Lady Melbourne [i.e., the mother of Cecil's hero] had contrived to weld them together into that strongest of social units, a compact family group; with its own standards, its own idiom of thought and speech, its own jokes; confronting the world with the cheerful confidence that, where it differed from others, it was right and the others were wrong" (36–37). Save for the one proper noun, not a syllable need be changed in order to describe the micro-civilization that Rose and Joseph Kennedy constructed for themselves and their nine children. Or again, here is Cecil's most succinct description of his hero: "He was a sceptic in thought, in practice a hedonist" (76). Once more, this is Kennedy. He was never strongly attached to any ideology except anti-communism, and during his presidency he began somewhat to doubt even that, at least in its more severe, hardline versions; and JFK generally regarded with (sometimes amused) superiority those who did not share his skepticism toward all certainties. Like Melbourne, he was also a practicing hedonist. Though a weak stomach often made it difficult for him to enjoy rich food or strong drink, he took whatever sensual pleasures he could—from fine cigars to the sexual favors of gorgeous Hollywood actresses.

Some of the parallels between Melbourne and Kennedy are almost eerie. Melbourne had a mentally disabled son, as Kennedy had a mentally disabled sister. Melbourne had a daughter who died at birth, as Kennedy had a stillborn daughter and a son who died after two days of life. Yet more strikingly, the political careers of the two men were both, in very similar ways, accidental. William Lamb was his parents' second son. He had no expectation of inheriting the viscountcy, and in his youth looked forward to a leisurely private life that would combine pleasant socializing with intellectual and literary pursuits. When, however, his older brother Peniston died of consumption, William had little choice but to take up the political career that, as Cecil explains, was all but mandatory for the eldest sons of the great Whig families. He eventually rose to the top of his profession, serving seven years as prime minister. John Kennedy was also a second son, and seems to have envisioned a career devoted to studying and writing about history, government, and political philosophy. He was extremely proud that his senior thesis at Harvard was not only published as a book (*Why England*

Slept [1940]) but became a bestseller. But Joseph Kennedy had once harbored presidential ambitions for himself, and, when these came to nothing, he determined that his eldest son should succeed where he had failed. After Joseph Kennedy Jr. (JFK's older brother) was killed in World War II, JFK was unable to resist his family's determination that he pursue a path leading to the White House.

Of course, there were differences between Melbourne and Kennedy too; yet even within the differences there were similarities. Their marriages, for instance, were unalike. Caroline Ponsonby Lamb was a woman of wild recklessness. She was committed to a romantic rebelliousness most scandalously expressed by an extensive series of highly public extramarital love affairs, with men ranging from her family's doctor to the poet Lord Byron, the most popular literary celebrity of the age.[19] Jacqueline Bouvier Kennedy, by contrast, behaved with impeccable propriety. Only 31 years old when she became First Lady, and subjected to more intense scrutiny than perhaps any other woman in American history to that point, she committed hardly a single misstep during the entirety of the Kennedy Administration. But there were parallels between the two women too. Blessed with extreme physical attractiveness, both women became national icons of beauty, elegance, and charm. If the term "sex symbol" had been invented in the nineteenth century, and if it could be applied to anyone of such irreproachable dignity as Jackie Kennedy, it would be an appropriate description of both women. Perhaps it is more than an interesting coincidence that John Kennedy named his daughter Caroline.

It is, of course, impossible to know exactly to what degree Cecil's book inspired Kennedy to take Melbourne as a model. But it is hard to resist the suspicion that its influence on his career was considerable. In any case, the specifically political and ideological comparisons between Melbourne and Kennedy are especially interesting and important. Though a Whig (mainly out of loyalty to family tradition), and despite a youthful admiration for the radical Whig leader Charles James Fox, Melbourne was an instinctive conservative at heart. He was never a reactionary—he was firmly opposed to the extreme Tories—but he did tend to feel that the way things happened to be were probably about the best they could be: not a surprising attitude for one who spent his whole life in an environment of great luxury and privilege. In addition, his general skepticism made him wary of most schemes for the improvement of humanity's lot. As Cecil summarizes Melbourne's mature outlook:

> No, life was an insoluble conundrum; and all that a sensible man could do was to try and get through it with as little unpleasantness to himself, and everyone else, as possible; in private to be considerate and detached, in public to do what little he could to guide the world down its uncharted course with the minimum of friction. This generally involved doing very little. It certainly meant refusing to risk an immediate disturbance for the sake of a problematical future good.
>
> (262)

In his dealings with Queen Victoria (with whom he often spent several hours a day and who provided him with his own private apartment in Windsor Castle), Melbourne generally attempted to guide her toward the tried and conventional. He might almost be called more "Victorian" than Victoria herself.

"Doing very little": Superficially, that certainly sounds unlike the John Kennedy who in 1960 campaigned to "get America moving again," and who always upheld "vigor" as a cherished ideal. JFK was fascinated by what the political-science textbooks of the day called the "strong president"—a partly imaginary amalgam of elements drawn mainly from the presidencies of Jackson, Lincoln, Woodrow Wilson, and both Roosevelts—and he hoped that historians would someday apply the epithet to him. Yet there would be some real truth—though also a little unfairness—in saying that Kennedy was more attached to the *idea* of doing great things than to actually doing them.

The gibe is less than completely fair because the Kennedy Administration, though truncated as it was, did manage some genuine achievements. The Peace Corps and the Partial Nuclear Test Ban Treaty of 1963 are important examples. It should also be remembered that Kennedy campaigned in 1960 for a number of domestic reforms that, by the standards of today, sound hair-raisingly radical. He advocated expanding the Social Security system to include medical insurance for the elderly (the idea that, after his death, became Medicare). He protested that President Eisenhower had allowed the construction of public housing to stall, and said that two million new units should be built annually. In a country where K-12 education had always been regarded as a local, and, to a lesser degree, a state responsibility, Kennedy advocated direct federal aid to the nation's public schools, with some money earmarked for teachers' salaries. It is a bit difficult to imagine Lord Melbourne wholly approving of such things, which do not really amount to "doing very little."

Yet in many ways there was less to Kennedy's apparent activism than meets the eye. His proposals seem radical to us today because we still (though perhaps decreasingly) live in the conservative era inaugurated by the Reagan Administration and ratified by the Clinton Administration. "The era of big government is over," as Bill Clinton famously proclaimed, expressly repudiating the tradition of the New Deal. But in 1960 the New Deal was agreed common sense for the great majority of Democrats (many of the Southerners excepted). What Kennedy proposed might well have been advocated by any Democratic nominee for the presidency: and, quite likely, by most of them with more enthusiasm than Kennedy himself managed to summon. For, when JFK won the nomination in July 1960, his record in the US Senate was arguably the most conservative of almost any Northeastern Democrat. He necessarily made gestures in a liberal direction—after all, Lyndon Johnson, his chief rival for the nomination, had sewn up the support of most of the conservative Southern wing of the party—but never seemed entirely comfortable doing so. The liberals, for their part, though they eventually came to accept Kennedy, never completely trusted him; and he was certainly not their first choice for the presidential nomination. They much preferred Hubert Humphrey and, after Humphrey's campaign ended in defeat, Adlai Stevenson. It is symptomatic that Eleanor Roosevelt—at that time the grand matriarch of Democratic Party liberalism and the most important living link to her husband's New Deal—and JFK never got along at all well with one another.[20] The reliably left-liberal literary and political critic Irving Howe, though writing in the immediate aftermath of the assassination, and acknowledging his share in the grief that was then overwhelming the nation, felt obliged to point out, truthfully, that JFK "was not a firm or innovating liberal, and what is more, he did not particularly claim to be. It was only his friends and his guests who made that claim."[21]

It was with regard to the most important moral and social crisis during the period of Kennedy's presidency—the civil rights movement—that Kennedy's Melbourne-like conservatism was most telling. The history here is complicated, and needs to be recalled in a little detail. During his career in Congress, Kennedy had never been identified with the cause of civil rights. In this, he was unlike many Northern Democrats (such as Humphrey) and, indeed, unlike Republican Vice-President Richard Nixon, who was extravagantly praised by Martin Luther King for his role in the passage of the Civil Rights Act of 1957 (which Kennedy voted to weaken). But things changed dramatically in October 1960, at the height of the closely contested presidential campaign. On the basis of an obscure traffic technicality, the authorities in Georgia sentenced Dr. King to four months in prison—apparently with the intention of having King murdered while in custody (he presumably would have been "shot while trying to escape"). King's family frantically appealed to the Nixon campaign for help, and, when none was forthcoming, they decided to try the Kennedy campaign instead. JFK made a phone call of support and sympathy to Mrs. King, and Robert Kennedy, who was managing his older brother's campaign, called the judge handling the case. King was soon released, and Kennedy instantly became a civil rights hero. King's father, the Rev. Martin Luther King Sr., called a highly publicized press conference to announce that, though he had been supporting Nixon because of Kennedy's Catholicism, he was now reversing himself and strongly backing Kennedy for president.[22]

So, when JFK entered the White House in January 1961, expectations that he would show real leadership on civil rights were high. His actual performance was anything but a profile in courage. To be sure, there seems little question that JFK was personally opposed to white racism: though, in his detached Melbournian way, probably less because he found it morally repugnant than because he thought it stupid and irrational, a pointless waste of energy and resources. Kennedy shuddered inwardly during conversations with Harry Truman—the only living Democrat to have preceded him in the White House, who had a habit of ranting about "niggers"—and he once ordered that his entire campaign entourage be moved from a Kentucky hotel when it refused accommodations to a black reporter.[23] But JFK's personal feelings about race were one thing. The realities of American politics were quite another. Like all the other Democrats who had been elected to the presidency since the Civil War—the grand total before Kennedy was only four—JFK had depended on the electoral votes of the so-called "Solid South." Yet there had been and were clear signs that the solidity of Democratic support in the South was eroding. As early as 1948, many Southerners bolted their party because of a civil rights plank in the party platform; and the arch-segregationist Strom Thurmond of South Carolina, running for president that year as a "Dixiecrat," carried four Deep South states. In the 1950s, Eisenhower—a national war hero whose appeal somewhat transcended party and region—carried Virginia, Tennessee, and Florida twice, Louisiana once. In 1960, Nixon carried the same three Southern states that Eisenhower had taken both times; and, perhaps even more ominously, Mississippi and Alabama—previously the two most safely Democratic states in the nation—gave fourteen of their electoral votes not to Kennedy but to the segregationist Senator Harry Byrd of Virginia. The times, they were a-changing.

It was clear, then, that (as Franklin Roosevelt had recognized a generation earlier) race and civil rights were the one issue that could shatter the Solid South and put the White House out of reach for the Democrats. For, other things being equal, there was simply no way that a Democrat could put together a reliable majority in the Electoral College without near-unanimous or at least overwhelming support from the states of the Old Confederacy. In electoral terms, of course, the South meant the white South. Not only were whites (then as now) a clear majority in every Southern state, but, outside of certain large cities, Southern blacks were generally prevented from voting by a combination of bureaucratic obstruction and open physical terror. White Southerners were thus crucial to Kennedy's re-election in 1964.

This is the context in which JFK's instincts on civil rights tended toward (to recall Melbourne's general stance as paraphrased by Cecil) "refusing to risk an immediate disturbance for the sake of a problematical future good."[24] One of the clearest examples of his presumptive conservatism concerned racial discrimination in federally supported housing. In the course of the second debate with Nixon during the 1960 campaign, Kennedy pointed out that such discrimination could and should be ended without involving Congress at all. It could be done by executive order, or, as he put it, "by a stroke of the president's pen." Many of those who voted for Kennedy may well have thought that the appropriate stroke would come on inauguration day. But it did not. JFK procrastinated and delayed, as increasingly disappointed civil rights leaders hit on a nicely sarcastic gesture and mailed hundreds of pens to the White House. In November 1962, two full years after being elected, the president did, finally, issue the fair-housing order.

Much the same pattern obtained in the more dramatic civil rights crises of the early 1960s. In May 1961, for example, several groups of black and white civil rights workers constituted themselves as the "Freedom Riders," availing themselves of the rights granted by a recent Supreme Court decision that had outlawed racial segregation in interstate buses and in the terminal facilities (waiting rooms, restaurants, toilets) that served them. In the Deep South, the Freedom Riders—American citizens travelling peacefully through their own country—were met by white mobs that, with the tacit or not-so-tacit support of local all-white police forces, beat and bombed them. Kennedy was furious—at the Freedom Riders. "Can't you get your goddamned friends off those buses?" he thundered to Harris Wofford—JFK's only important aide who unequivocally supported civil rights for African Americans, and whom he sometimes seemed to hold personally responsible for the entire civil rights movement.[25] Kennedy's emphasis was on trying to make the whole issue somehow go away. He declined to use military troops to protect the lives of Americans (as Eisenhower in 1957 had sent the 82nd Airborne to Little Rock, Arkansas, during a school desegregation crisis—a move opposed by then-Senator Kennedy). Instead, he sent a small group of federal "marshals": actually a miscellaneous collection of unarmed and mostly middle-aged officials from various federal departments. Their courage was undeniable, but the ineffectiveness of Kennedy's response is suggested by the fact that the "marshal" whom JFK designated as his personal representative on the scene—a Justice Department employee and assistant to Attorney General Robert Kennedy named John Seigenthaler, himself a white Southerner—wound up beaten and bloody in an Alabama hospital. Martin Luther King, who half a year earlier had expressed gratitude to JFK for helping him get out of jail, now privately denounced the Kennedy brothers for betraying the cause of civil rights.

And so it went, for the most part, during the subsequent civil rights crises. There was the desegregation of the University of Mississippi in September 1962, during which the federal officials did have firearms but were strictly ordered by the president not to use them against the violent white mobs even to save their own lives. There were the civil rights demonstrations in Birmingham, Alabama, in May 1963, where black marchers, including many children, were sensationally brutalized by the violently racist Bull Connor, for many years head of the city's police and fire departments. Kennedy's response was so tepid that it was denounced by his own appointee to the federal Civil Rights Commission, Dean Erwin Griswold of the Harvard Law School. Perhaps most important of all, there was the great March for Jobs and Freedom in Washington, DC, in August 1963, at which Martin Luther King gave his famous "I Have a Dream" speech. John and Robert Kennedy did everything they could to prevent the march from taking place, and, when they failed, JFK pointedly declined an invitation to address the marchers himself.

Kennedy always refused simply to surrender to the often violent lawlessness of the Southern segregationists. But he also refused, for the most part, to place the moral, political, and legal authority of his office squarely on the side of the civil rights movement. He kept trying to have it both ways, appearing friendly enough to civil rights to appease his liberal constituency represented by people like Harris Wofford, and yet not so friendly that in 1964 he would sacrifice the electoral votes of the states of the Old Confederacy. His favorite gambit was to present himself as constitutionally bound by his oath of office, which obliged him to take care that the laws of the United States be faithfully executed. When the federal courts had issued their binding interpretations as to what the federal law required, the president—as Kennedy explained more than once— had no choice but to enforce their judgments, regardless of his personal opinions on the matter. This may well have been a case in which the attempt to please everybody wound up really pleasing nobody. The civil rights movement generally viewed the Kennedy Administration as a disappointment, while the hard-core Southern segregationists bitterly hated John Kennedy (and, even more, his brother Robert) as they had never hated any important national Democrats before (save perhaps Eleanor Roosevelt). But it is easy to imagine Lord Melbourne understanding and admiring JFK's aversion to "risking immediate disturbances."

Kennedy's Melbournian conservatism should also be examined in his approach to foreign and military policy, matters more directly relevant to Stone's *JFK* than the domestic crises over civil rights. Before doing so, however, I will analyze the film itself. For reasons directly related to the misrepresentations of the film in the unparalleled journalistic campaign of defamation against it, it will be useful, first of all, to consider *JFK* by way of certain crucial cinematic influences upon it. Though Stone's innovative editing techniques owe much to Sergei Eisenstein and Jean-Luc Godard, I will concentrate here on what might be called the film's epistemological structure: which can best be approached in the light of two major precursor-films by Akira Kurosawa and Orson Welles, respectively.

Precursor-Texts: *Rashomon* and *Citizen Kane*

Rashomon (Akira Kurosawa, 1950) is, like *JFK,* about a crime. As with *JFK,* a few basic facts about the crime are clear enough, while most of the details in which we might be interested remain frustratingly obscure. What is clear in Stone's film is that President Kennedy was shot to death in Dealey Plaza on November 22, 1963. What is clear in Kurosawa's film is that, in a dark forest near Kyoto, Japan, sometime in the eleventh century, a notorious bandit (Toshirô Mifune) raped a beautiful noblewoman (Machiko Kyô), and that, somehow as a result of this rape, the woman's husband, a samurai (Masayuki Mori), wound up dead. The bandit, the woman, and (speaking through a medium from beyond the grave) the husband all give their separate accounts of exactly what happened. A fourth account is given by an ordinary woodcutter (Takashi Shimura), who was not directly involved in the crime but who happened to witness it while roaming the forest in order to gather wood.

These accounts—shown at some length in flashbacks—all vary considerably from one another. For example, the bandit explains the samurai's death by saying that, after the rape, the woman, feeling deeply shamed, asked him to fight her husband to the death so that only one living man would know of her "dishonor." The two men do battle, and the husband is killed in a fair fight. But the husband insists that he killed *himself*, after hearing that his wife had not only agreed to run away with her rapist—who had been professing great love for her—but had also implored the bandit to kill him (the husband). The wife herself says that she begged her husband to forgive her for having been raped, but that he only gazed at her with cold loathing—whereupon she became so upset that she fainted, only to find her husband stabbed to death when she awakened. The woodcutter's version, whose story might be supposed to be the most "objective," differs from all the others. He remembers that the wife savagely condemned *both* her husband and the bandit as not "real men," and encouraged the two men to fight. They do so, and the samurai is killed—as in the bandit's version, though the details of the fight are very different. Given that the film is structured on such epistemological indeterminacy, it is quite appropriate that the first line of dialog, spoken by the woodcutter, should be, "I don't understand, I just don't understand"—and that another character later comments (perhaps speaking for the typical viewer), "The more I hear, the more confused I get."[26]

There are many other discrepancies among the four stories. But the uncertainties of the film are not a function *only* of the variance among the competing narratives. Even within a particular version, things are not always quite clear. For instance, who, in the wife's version, actually killed the samurai? Many commentators have assumed that it was the wife herself, who presumably fainted after doing the deed and who, perhaps, had repressed the memory when she awoke. This assumption would make for a nice symmetry among the stories by the three principals, with each of the latter claiming to have killed the samurai. Yet this assumption is not confirmed by anything we actually see in the wife's flashback; and it is arguably contradicted by the wife's insistence that she was horribly shocked to find her husband dead. The husband might have killed himself while his wife was unconscious; or the bandit (who in the wife's telling left the scene very shortly after the rape) might have come back and stabbed the samurai. We should also note that it is not only the narratives of the film that produce the unclarity of which the woodcutter complains, but the cinematography as well. The flashbacks that display the crime are all set in a dense forest where it is difficult to see anything with complete lucidity; sunlight is filtered through a thick panoply of tree branches and leaves. Likewise, during the time present of the film, when the woodcutter and several other characters discuss the crime, a hard rain falls, also hindering our vision.

Rashomon is a landmark in movie history in several ways. It won both the Grand Prix at the prestigious Venice Film Festival and an Oscar for Best Foreign Film, effectively introducing not only Kurosawa himself but Japanese cinema as a whole to the West. It also introduced an overt kind of epistemological uncertainty to world cinema. The centrally structuring formal device of *Rashomon* is related to, but also significantly different from, the unreliable narrator that had long been familiar in prose fiction. The unreliable prose narrator does not greatly outrage common sense, because common sense has long admitted that we should not always believe everything that people tell us: whether because the teller is morally untrustworthy (like Humbert Humbert, who narrates Vladimir Nabokov's *Lolita* [1955]), or because the teller is incapable of fully understanding the events described (like the title character who narrates Mark Twain's *Huckleberry Finn* [1884]). But common sense typically *does* hold—and this is the principle that caused so much confusion among the political journalists who savaged *JFK*—that "seeing is believing." Cinema is of course an art based primarily on seeing; and one's natural assumption tends to be that what one sees is actually there. If, in *Rashomon*, the four informants had merely *told* their competing versions of the crime, we would not be at all surprised to find discrepancies among the tellings. But, because each tale is not only told but visually dramatized in flashback—because, for example, we *see* the wife humbly begging her husband's forgiveness but also see her bitterly denouncing him—the effect is very different. In 1950, audiences were accustomed to assume that anything actually shown on screen—and not expressly presented as dream, or daydream, or hallucination, or outright lie, or anything else of the sort—corresponded to physical reality within the fictionality of the film. *Rashomon* shattered that expectation, and in so doing proved enormously influential. There have been at least dozens and more probably hundreds of movies and television programs structured in direct emulation of Kurosawa's film. Indeed, the film's influence has extended even beyond the art of cinema. At least in the United States, attorneys and detectives often refer to "the *Rashomon* effect" to mean the (not uncommon) situation in which eyewitnesses give conflicting testimony about the same event. Stone himself has acknowledged *Rashomon* as a crucial influence on *JFK*.[27]

Yet the real innovation of *Rashomon* was that the unreliability of action shown on screen is explicitly thematized into the principal point of the film. As we have seen, Kurosawa's film announces its real "subject matter" in its first spoken line, "I don't understand, I just don't understand." *Rashomon* was not, however, the first film to problematize the commonsense assumption that seeing is believing. Made nine years earlier, *Citizen Kane* (Orson Welles, 1941) has had an even greater influence, both on cinema in general and on the work of Oliver Stone in particular.

Unlike *JFK* and *Rashomon*, Welles's movie presents the investigation not of a crime but of something subtler and more nebulous. The investigation—primarily undertaken by the virtually anonymous journalist Thompson (William Alland), who is generally seen with his back to the camera—nominally focuses on the dying utterance of the American newspaper magnate Charles Foster Kane (Welles himself), the now legendary single word, "Rosebud." More substantially, though, the search is really not so much for the meaning of those two syllables as for the meaning of Kane's life and career as a whole.

As in *Rashomon*, a number of quite different answers are given. The "News on the March" newsreel at the beginning of *Citizen Kane*—the documentary film within the fiction film—presents Kane in the style of "objective" journalism, emphasizing the tycoon's wealth and power and the fascination he always held for his fellow Americans. Shortly after the newsreel ends, we meet the man's second wife, Susan Alexander Kane (Dorothy Comingore), too sunk in alcohol and depression to be able to convey much of anything at all—but we will be meeting her again. The next version of Kane is given, in flashback, by an unpublished manuscript left by the late Walter Parks Thatcher (George Courlouris), an immensely wealthy Wall Street financier who raised Kane from boyhood to adulthood after Kane's originally modest circumstances were radically altered when his mother came into possession of one of the world's richest gold mines. Thatcher has already been seen in the newsreel, condemning Kane as essentially a communist (a labor leader has also been seen, condemning Kane as a fascist). His own manuscript, however, stresses not just Kane's political ideology but, even more, his general aggressivity, arrogance, and exasperating personal qualities. But Thatcher is soon denounced as "the biggest darn fool," who never understood Kane at all, by the next informant, Mr. Bernstein (Everett Sloane), Kane's long-time general manager. After Kane's death, he has taken over as the chairman of the board of the late multimillionaire's business empire. Bernstein's flashback offers a hero-worshipper's view of Kane: The tycoon is seen as principled and dedicated, and also as irresistibly attractive and charismatic. It is through Bernstein's eyes that we see Kane as the idealistic author of the "Declaration of Principles," pledging to use his journalistic influence to defend the rights of the common people. Bernstein also shows us Kane at his most physically magnetic, and with an appeal that is somewhat androgynous in form. In the great musical scene where Kane joins a dancing chorus line to help perform a song recently composed about him, he at some points seems a hypermasculine conqueror, implicitly claiming sexual rights (and sexual power) over a whole floor full of attractive and scantily clad young women. But at other points he seems more like one of the girls himself.

Bernstein's version is answered by the longest of the flashbacks, that which dramatizes the story offered by Jedediah Leland (Joseph Cotten), the best friend of Kane's youth who eventually fell out with him. At the beginning, Jedediah's memory of Kane is not very different from Bernstein's. But, as time passes, Jed—unlike Bernstein— sees the beautiful, graceful, slender young man to have aged into pompous, heavyset middle age in a way that parallels Kane's transformation from a youthful progressive idealist to the increasingly conservative plutocrat who is motivated by little beyond his lust for more and more personal power. In the most incisive explicit critique that anyone offers of Kane throughout the film, an intoxicated but lucid Jedediah suggests to Kane, just after the latter has lost an election (apparently for the governorship of New York), that his professed progressive populism was never really genuine at all. Kane, says Jed, cared for the common people only to the extent that he could see them as his dependents and himself as the patron who would "give" them their rights: and Kane's unhappy conservative turn has been mainly an effect of the growing realization that democratic politics cannot really work that way. This view coheres rather neatly with the version of Kane offered in the following flashback, the one from Susan's point of view. In her second interview with Thompson, she proves more forthcoming, and portrays Kane as being just as controlling, self-absorbed, and manipulative in marriage as Jedediah had suggested him to be on the political stage. The final version of Kane is offered by his butler Raymond (Paul Stewart)—evidently the only person who actually heard him say, "Rosebud"—who recalls him as a pathetic, lonely, out-of-control old man.[28]

In contrast to *Rashomon*—and in a way that, as we will see, bears some important affinity to the structure of *JFK*—none of the competing narratives of *Citizen Kane* flatly contradicts any of the others on the plane of mere fact. The relation among all the versions of Kane is exceedingly complex, the different stories sometimes (as with Susan's and Jed's) dovetailing smoothly with one another, sometimes (as with Jed's and Bernstein's) relating to each other with considerable tension. The ultimate implication of the movie *in toto* may be that all the various narratives contain some elements of truth, but that none of them by itself, nor even all of them put together, reveal the whole truth. There is an irreducible margin of mystery, of enigma, about that very outgoing public man, Charles Foster Kane—just as, in *JFK*, the assassination (which, in a way, is almost a character itself) remains in many respects beyond our or the film's grasp. It is thus appropriate that, at the very end of the film, when the viewer (unlike the hapless Thompson) finally does discover the meaning of "Rosebud"—that it was the brand name of a toy sled that Kane possessed as a small boy and that he used to strike Thatcher when Thatcher first came to take the young Charles away to live with him—the revelation explains hardly anything at all about Kane's life and death. This refusal of the closure that we may have been expecting is deeply akin to the ultimate stance of *JFK*.

JFK: Conspiracy

Oliver Stone is generally considered the most technically versatile and accomplished American filmmaker of his generation; and the technical virtuosity of *JFK* has been all but unanimously acknowledged by film scholars like Roger Ebert. The Academy, though it declined to name the film as Best Picture of its year or Stone as Best Director—not to mention several other Oscar nominations that the film earned but that were not consummated by actual awards—did, as we have seen, for once know what it was doing when it bestowed its prizes for Best Cinematography and Best Film Editing. The perhaps unprecedented complexity of the film's technical composition—with the extreme heterogeneity of its visual representations, and its more than two hundred speaking parts—is indispensable for producing the film's open-ended epistemological structure, the refusal of conceptual closure that it inherits from *Citizen Kane* and *Rashomon*: and this element of philosophical indeterminacy is, in turn, integral to the view that *JFK* takes toward what it assumes to be the conspiracy that murdered President Kennedy.

One important aspect of the film's technical versatility is the variety and varied origins of footage used. *JFK* contains 8mm, 16mm, 35mm, and Super 8 film stock, plus some video footage. Most of the footage is in color, but much is in black and white. Most includes synchronized sound, but some is silent. Numerous still photographs are embedded in this motion picture, and, though most of the movie is fictional footage shot by Stone, a not unimportant fraction is composed of nonfictional archival footage. One bit of archival footage is especially important. In the portions of the film that dramatize events directly related to Kennedy's assassination (as opposed to events in or related to Garrison's investigation of the crime), the closest thing we ever have to a baseline "objective" reality—to a version of the murder that is presented with a near-absolute degree of epistemological confidence—is produced by some archival footage from what must count as the most consequential "home movie" in American history: the so-called "Zapruder film."

Abraham Zapruder was an immigrant Dallas businessman of Russian-Jewish background, who, as a Democrat and an admirer of President Kennedy, decided, on November 22, 1963, to take his then-state-of-the-art 8mm Bell & Howell home movie camera to Dealey Plaza in order to record the presidential visit to his city. Standing on an elevated concrete abutment, Zapruder exposed 486 frames of silent Kodachrome color film, capturing 26.6 seconds of the presidential motorcade, including the assassination itself. The early parts of the film are quite ordinary. We see Kennedy seated next to his wife, who is wearing a beautiful pink outfit, in the back seat of an open-top car. At one point the president is apparently chatting with John Connally, then the governor of Texas, who is sitting directly in front of him. But the later seconds are those that have become part of history and that are highlighted in *JFK*: the shots hitting the president, including the fatal head shot at frame 313, and Jackie Kennedy immediately afterward climbing onto the back of the car. When Garrison, in real life, displayed the Zapruder film at the 1969 trial of Clay Shaw for conspiracy to murder President Kennedy, it was the first time that the film had been seen in public (Time Inc., to which Zapruder had sold the copyright, kept it locked away for the previous six years). By the time that *JFK* appeared, the Zapruder film had been publicly shown on a number of occasions; but Stone's use of it (mainly though not exclusively in the scenes dramatizing Garrison's use of it in the courtroom) provided the Zapruder film with probably its largest audience to that point. It has since become much more widely available, and today is easily accessible on the Internet.[29]

Diegetically, the Zapruder film is used in *JFK* mainly to illustrate some of Garrison's theories of the Kennedy assassination. But its larger, extra-diegetic significance is to provide us with something that, amidst all the murkiness and unanswered questions that surround the Kennedy assassination, we can actually be sure of. With the Zapruder film (which Garrison, at one point in the film, describes to an assistant as something that the conspirators had failed to foresee), seeing really *is* believing. We can have no doubt that Kennedy was in that slow-moving car travelling through Dealey Plaza, that he was seated next to Jackie Kennedy and directly behind Governor Connally, and that he was shot to death. The Zapruder film provides us with the same kind of certainty that, in *Rashomon*, we possess in knowing that the bandit raped the woman and that the samurai, somehow as a result, suffered a violent death. As embedded within *JFK*, the Zapruder film in one way corresponds to the "News on the March" newsreel in *Citizen Kane*: for Welles's movie never allows us to doubt that, for all the uncertainties and complexities that surround his character, Charles Foster Kane was indeed, as the newsreel makes clear, one of the richest, most powerful, and most fascinating Americans of his time. The authenticity of the Zapruder film has never been questioned, in real life, by those who have investigated the Kennedy assassination. Nor does Stone's movie, within its fictionality, permit any such doubt of its genuineness.

So we can believe, unproblematically, the veracity of the frames of the Zapruder film that *JFK* shares with us. But the same is true of very little of the non-archival footage in the parts of Stone's movie that represent events directly related to the murder of the president. Contrary to what was assumed by the journalists who attacked the film after watching it carelessly or not at all, *JFK* stresses just how much uncertainty surrounds the assassination of its titular character: and, as in *Rashomon*, the fact that we see something on screen is hardly any guarantee of its veracity.

The film begins with an epigraph from the writings of the once widely popular American poet Ella Wheeler Wilcox ("To sin by silence when we should protest makes cowards out of men"), and then—over and among the opening credits—presents us, in an all but explicit allusion to *Citizen Kane*, with its own newsreel. The latter features President Eisenhower delivering his famous Farewell Address, in which he warns of the dangers of the military-industrial complex; and it then offers a brief account (about six minutes) of the Kennedy presidency, from his narrow victory over Nixon in the 1960 election to the assassination in Dallas. (We later see Kennedy's death being announced to the nation by Walter Cronkite in a special television report from CBS News. Cronkite's coverage of the Kennedy assassination and its aftermath became the most cele-brated chapter in a long and widely celebrated journalistic career; perhaps a proprietary attitude toward the assassination helped to motivate Cronkite's verbal assault on Roger Ebert.) The voice-over narration is clearly written for the film and, in contrast to the studied "objectivity" of the newsreel in *Citizen Kane*, suggests in somewhat understated fashion the admiring view of Kennedy that will be developed in the film as a whole. But all the visual footage appears to be nonfictional and archival, save a very little dramatic reconstruction of actual events and perhaps a few mood-setting but factually inconsequential shots that might as well be archival.

There is, however, one important exception. In the first signifi-cant fictional footage to appear in *JFK*, we see, in black and white a little more than four minutes into the film, a young-to-middle-aged woman (played by Sally Kirkland) being thrown from a moving car onto the side of a rural highway. We next see her in a hospital bed, warning that "they"—never identified more specifically than as "serious fucking guys"—are planning to murder Kennedy. The medical personnel standing by her bedside do not seem interested in what she is saying, and one comments, "She's high as a kite on something." The woman is not named at this point in the film, but any viewer possessing fairly detailed knowledge of the scholarship on the Kennedy assassination would recognize her as (presumably) Rose Cheramie (which is how she is once referred to later and how she is identified in the credits). On November 20, 1963, Cheramie was indeed found by the side of highway 190 near Eunice, Louisiana, and was taken to a nearby hospital with relatively superficial injuries (evidently caused, however, by being hit by a car rather than by being thrown out of one). According to some reports, Cheramie claimed to have worked as a stripper and a drug runner for Jack Ruby—the Dallas nightclub owner who on November 24, 1963, murdered Lee Oswald—and did warn of the imminent Kennedy assassination. In *JFK*, the black-and-white footage of Rose Cheramie is intercut with (mainly color) archival news footage representing Kennedy's visit to Dallas. The intercutting tends to lend the brief narrative of Cheramie some of the authority of the (mostly quite familiar) nonfictional footage, which includes portions of the Zapruder film; and this authority is greatly enhanced by the fact that the Cheramie footage seems to be presented simply as itself, as "objective" reality, rather than as the memory or speculation of any particular character. In this movie that raises so many more questions than it attempts to answer, it seems fair, then, to take it as the considered position of *JFK*, established in less than five minutes of running time, that there *are* unanswered questions surrounding the Kennedy assassination, and that the murder was probably the work of a conspiracy: a conspiracy, that is, of "serious fucking guys."

But *which* guys, exactly? Contrary to the misapprehensions of the political journalists who mounted the defamatory campaign against *JFK*, the movie never really presumes to answer this question with precision and confidence. At the same time, it does not go quite so far in the direction of epistemological skepticism as *Rashomon*. The closer comparison, in this context, is with *Citizen Kane*. Welles's film offers to convey a great deal about Charles Foster Kane, while, at the same time, declining to claim that its set of representations is unproblematic or exhaustive. "Rosebud," one might say, is not simply the brand name of a toy sled, but also, and more importantly, a kind of Lévi-Straussian "floating signifier" that possesses no completely determinate content—it is a signifier that is securely anchored to no particular signified—and that thereby serves as a stand-in for everything we do *not* know about Kane. Likewise, *JFK* proposes that President Kennedy was murdered by conspiracy: the conspiracy of which the injured woman warns at the beginning of the film, and the existence of which Garrison, in his summation to the jury at the trial of Clay Shaw, offers to prove by demonstrating that the Warren Commission's lone-gunman theory of the assassination is ballistically impossible. Furthermore, the film, by the end, does, as we will see, roughly establish a very general hypothesis as to the nature of the conspiracy. Yet nearly every detail is uncertain: Every informant upon whom Garrison relies is as problematic as the witnessing characters of Kurosawa or Welles. Leaving aside the archival footage supplied by Abraham Zapruder and the network news divisions, *JFK* plunges us into a world of massive epistemological indeterminacy.

For instance, one of the first people that the film's Garrison interviews after beginning his investigation in 1966—itself launched in large part as a result of a conversation with Senator Russell Long (Walter Matthau), who scorns the lone-gunman theory of the assassination—is one Jack Martin (Jack Lemmon). Martin, we are informed, was a long-time associate of Guy Bannister (Ed Asner), an extreme-right-wing former FBI agent and private investigator based in New Orleans. As Martin tells it, his job in Bannister's office during the summer of 1963 was to handle ordinary private-detective work, while the rest of the office—including Bannister himself—devoted most of their time to something called

"Operation Mongoose": a CIA-linked effort to prepare for a second invasion of Cuba that would succeed in overthrowing the Castro government after the one in 1961 at the Bay of Pigs failed. According to Martin, among those prominent in Bannister's office were David Ferrie (Joe Pesci)—a failed candidate for the Catholic priesthood, a former Eastern Airlines pilot, and a trainer of anti-Castro mercenaries, whom Garrison had interviewed and suspected immediately following the Kennedy assassination—and Lee Oswald (Gary Oldman), one of whose functions was apparently pretending to be a *pro*-Castro activist and to set up a New Orleans branch of the left-wing Fair Play for Cuba Committee. Martin also recalls seeing an elegant and apparently quite wealthy man whose identity he does not know but who, in the dramatization of Martin's story, is played by Tommy Lee Jones, who turns out to be, within the film's fictionality, the prominent New Orleans businessman Clay Shaw.

Though Martin recounts that Kennedy, following his agreement with the Soviet leader Nikita Khrushchev to resolve the Cuban Missile Crisis of 1962, ordered that Operation Mongoose be shut down, it is never exactly clear what, if anything, Martin's story has to do with the assassination. Martin keeps implying that there was some connection between Operation Mongoose and the murder of the president, and that he knows all sorts of interesting secrets (for example, that Bannister's own death may have been caused by something other and more sinister than the heart attack that was reported). But he is never forthright or completely explicit. Depressed and alcoholic (like Susan Alexander Kane in Welles's movie), he makes a dubiously credible witness at best.

Furthermore, the hints that Martin drops in his conversation with Garrison do not quite seem to agree with what we have seen of Martin and Bannister together earlier in the film. Martin's narrative as presented to Garrison (and to us) is evidently the dramatization of his own foggy and alcohol-sodden memories. The footage visually implies a considerable degree of uncertainty, with many very short takes, some jerky camera movements, and a few deliberately confusing extreme close-ups. But we have already seen, in more "objectively" presented footage, Martin and Bannister conversing on the day of the assassination itself. The footage here adopts a classically "realistic" Hollywood style, with muted colors and straightforward camera angles. The conversation between Martin and Bannister abruptly ends when Bannister comes to doubt—apparently for no good reason—Martin's loyalty to him, and savagely pistol-whips Martin with a .357 Magnum. Along the way, however, Bannister, who clearly knows Lee Oswald fairly well personally, expresses what appears to be spontaneous and sincere surprise that Oswald (as the news broadcasts report) killed the president whom Bannister detests. If, then, Bannister accepts the reports that incriminate Oswald for murder, and is genuinely surprised by the revelation, it casts some considerable doubt on—while not necessarily wholly discrediting—Martin's later implication that the men, like Bannister, behind Operation Mongoose were involved in the conspiracy to kill Kennedy.

Perhaps even more dubious than Martin is another of Garrison's informants, one Willie O'Keefe (Kevin Bacon). A fictional character rather than a historical figure—though partly based on at least four of the real-life Garrison's informants—O'Keefe is interviewed in prison, where he is serving time for male prostitution. Among O'Keefe's customers has been Clay Shaw (though O'Keefe knows him only under his alias, Clay Bertrand). O'Keefe describes his memories of a party at David Ferrie's residence in New Orleans in the late summer of 1963, at which those in attendance included Shaw, Oswald, Ferrie, and a number of right-wing Cubans. What O'Keefe remembers most vividly is a long, angry, and drunken political rant by Ferrie, who bitterly denounces Kennedy for closing down the camps at which mercenaries were training for Operation Mongoose, and who expresses a fierce desire to assassinate Castro (or perhaps to infect the Cuban leader with a poison that would make his beard fall out, a scheme actually considered, in real life, by the CIA). Prompted by one of the Cubans, Ferrie goes on to maintain that the way to get rid of Castro is to get rid of Kennedy first; and he insists that, despite the protection provided by the Secret Service and other law-enforcement agencies, Kennedy could be dispatched with relative ease. Ferrie even describes a plan for doing so in some detail, arguing, "Triangulation of crossfire—that's the key, that's the key": thus describing a *modus operandi* similar to that theorized in real life by most of those who have rejected the lone-gunman hypothesis of the Warren Report. As Ferrie raves on, Shaw—drinking but apparently not very drunk—seems uncomfortable with the conversation, and says, in his smooth, elegant voice, "Why don't we drop this subject? It's one thing to engage in badinage with all these youngsters, but this sort of thing could be *so* easily misunderstood." Shaw is clearly accepted by the others as the dominant member of the group, and the topic is indeed dropped. Throughout, Oswald has been quiet, while listening to Ferrie's oration with interest. There is a meaningful close-up of Oldman when Ferrie says that, as an indispensable part of the plot to kill Kennedy, one of the conspirators must be sacrificed.

What do we make of this? O'Keefe's dramatized story fits fairly well with Jack Martin's, but one does not in any way prove the other. The word of a convicted and imprisoned male prostitute is unlikely to carry much weight in a courtroom, as Garrison's assistant Bill Broussard (Michael Rooker), who has been present at the O'Keefe interview, points out to his boss. Within the fictionality of the film, however, the greater reason to doubt O'Keefe is that he turns out to be just as unhinged a right-wing fanatic as Ferrie himself. After relating the story of the party in reasonably calm, rational tones, O'Keefe launches into a furious diatribe against Kennedy that is as savage as Ferrie's own—though his interests seem to lie more in domestic than in foreign policy. He hates Kennedy for his civil rights policies (the way so many white Southerners, as we have seen, actually did), and for supposedly stealing the 1960 election from Nixon, who O'Keefe says would have been a great president, bringing a much needed fascism to America. O'Keefe wants the world to know that Kennedy was killed because (as O'Keefe believes) he was a communist; and he claims to be cooperating with Garrison because he cannot stand the thought that Oswald, whom he always disliked, should get all the credit for what he considers a wonderful deed.

And so it goes throughout *JFK*. That Kennedy was murdered by conspiracy—as suggested at the beginning by the desperate ravings of Rose Cheramie, and as increasingly established to a near-certainty, as the film unfolds, by what is repeatedly argued to be the physical impossibility of one shooter having been responsible for all the gunfire at Dealey Plaza—is not seriously in doubt. Yet every attempt to discover the details of the conspiracy plunges Garrison—and us—into a world of unreliable information and epistemological vertigo. The dramatizations of the stories that the various informants tell (always sharply distinct, visually, from the time-present footage in which they are embedded) are responsible for much of the film's power but also, in their evident unreliability, for much of the film's *Kane*-like and *Rashomon*-like uncertainty.

Indeed, though these visual dramatizations sometimes seem pretty clearly to illustrate a particular informant's words (as with the dramatization of O'Keefe's story of the party at Ferrie's house), at other times even their basic referentiality is much less certain. For instance, when Garrison interviews Shaw, prior to later indicting him, Shaw adamantly denies knowing either O'Keefe or Ferrie. Yet the time-present footage of Shaw and Garrison sitting and talking in Garrison's office is intercut with footage that shows Shaw and O'Keefe having dinner together in Shaw's luxurious French Quarter home and then participating in an elegantly decadent sado-masochistic homosexual orgy that also involves Ferrie (and one other man). Is this footage to be taken as representing

Shaw's actual—true—memory of the evening in question, even as he repeatedly lies about it to Garrison? Possibly. Yet it is at least equally plausible that the footage represents Garrison's imagining of what *might* have taken place, with numerous lurid details perhaps inspired by the anti-gay prejudice of which Garrison is later accused by his own wife: an accusation that he denies only perfunctorily and that might be taken to cohere fairly neatly with his own rather conventional masculinity. Tommy Lee Jones brilliantly portrays Shaw with a subtle undertone of danger and malice beneath a suave, controlled exterior; and there is little question that he is to be taken as a villain of some sort. But when we ask in what, *exactly*, his villainy consists, we once again receive no clear or reliable answers.

The informant who speaks at greatest length to Garrison is an individual of impressive deportment who summons the district attorney to Washington, where he identifies himself as a retired military man wishing to be known simply as "X" (he is played by Donald Sutherland). "X" is a fictional character (though generally considered to be partly based on Air Force Colonel Fletcher Prouty, who served as Chief of Special Operations for the Joint Chiefs of Staff during the Kennedy Administration, and who is credited as a technical adviser on *JFK*), and describes himself to Garrison as a long-time Pentagon specialist in so-called "Black Operations" or "Black Ops." These are secret, illegal US interventions in other countries by means of propaganda, psychological warfare, strike-breaking, the assassination of foreign leaders, the stealing of elections, *coups d'état* against foreign governments, and the like. "X" recounts a long series of successful Black Ops by himself and his colleagues in numerous countries, including Romania, Greece, Yugoslavia, Italy, France, the Philippines, Guatemala, Iran, Vietnam, Indonesia, and Tibet. "We were good—very good," says "X" with considerable pride in his voice. But this record of success was shattered by the failure of the invasion of Cuba at the Bay of

Pigs in 1961. Following that debacle, says "X," President Kennedy took a number of steps that caused great consternation within the US national-security establishment: among them the firing of CIA Director Allen Dulles and other top intelligence officials, the refusal to send US troops into Cuba in 1962, and the signing of the Partial Nuclear Test Ban Treaty in 1963. Most important of all was Kennedy's issuing, in the fall of 1963, of National Security Action Memorandum (NSAM) 263—on which "X" claims to have worked extensively—for the withdrawal of a thousand American troops from Vietnam by the end of 1964 and the withdrawal of the remainder by the end of 1965. When the assassination came in November 1963, "X" noticed a number of circumstances that have led him to believe that the murder of JFK was a Black Op by some of his old colleagues—with techniques developed for foreign interventions being brought home to the United States. Though he speaks in very broad terms, expressly declining to give specifics, what he seems to describe is a conspiracy directed by a small number of highly placed officials at the Pentagon and the CIA, who are sufficiently powerful to ensure the cooperation of lesser forces (like the Dallas Police Department) in covering up the conspiracy during the assassination's aftermath.

"X" speaks with the confidence, lucidity, and authoritative military bearing that might be expected in one of his purported background; and he certainly seems to be an informant on a level very different to that of an alcoholic Jack Martin, a raving unhinged David Ferrie, or a low-life racist Willie O'Keefe. At the same time, it is difficult to know exactly what to make of the extensive tutorial that he gives to Garrison. His own motivations are completely unclear. He has, as he says, resigned his military commission, but we do not know whether that is because he has come to disapprove of Black Ops on principle or—what he hints is more probably the case—simply because the failure of the United States to overthrow Castro and the horror of the Kennedy assassination have spoiled the enjoyment he had been accustomed to take in successful Black Ops. He presents himself to Garrison as an ally and strongly encourages the district attorney to continue his work. But he tells Garrison nothing that would be of any direct use in prosecuting a criminal case; and "X" emphatically refuses to offer testimony himself. One must even wonder whether "X" actually *has* resigned his commission as he claims to have done: for it is clearly suggested at more than one point in the film that nobody ever really leaves the intelligence agencies. By his own account, after all, "X" is a specialist in deception and manipulative psychological games; and it does not seem impossible that his meeting with Garrison is somehow itself part of yet another Black Op.

Aside, then, from confirming the film's consistent baseline assumption that JFK was murdered by conspiracy, "X" contributes nothing significant and specific to uncovering the *who* and the *how* of the assassination. Once again, we are as uncertain of the details of the Kennedy murder as we are of the details of the rape of the woman and the death of the samurai in Kurosawa's movie. "X" does, however, offer a quite coherent theory as to the *why* of Kennedy's death—which, as he himself says, is after all the most important question. Summing up what his years of military experience have taught him, "X" says: "The organizing principle of any society, Mr. Garrison, is for war. The authority of the state over its people resides in its war powers." Kennedy, he goes on, was killed because he intended to reduce the war powers of America's national-security state. His plan to withdraw from Vietnam would have deprived the military-industrial complex of the vast resources that, in the event, came into their possession after Kennedy's death and as a result of Lyndon Johnson's massive escalation and Americanization of the Vietnam War. Even more momentous, Kennedy—as "X" insists—intended to follow the Test Ban Treaty and the peaceful resolution of the Cuban Missile Crisis of 1962 with the actual ending, during his second term, of the Cold War with the Soviet Union.

Kennedy, says "X," intended to replace the competitive American-Soviet space race, for instance, with peaceful collaboration in the exploration of mankind's final frontier. Garrison, at first, is incredulous: "I can't believe they killed him because he wanted to change things. In our time, in our country!" "X" is merely amused by such *naïveté*: "They've been doing it throughout history," he says with a chuckle. "Kings are killed, Mr. Garrison. Politics is power, *nothing more.*"

Despite Garrison's initial incredulity—and despite the murkiness of his informant's real motives and intentions, and the refusal (or inability) of "X" to provide details about the Kennedy assassination that would be useful in a criminal prosecution—the district attorney generally adopts the political theory propounded by "X" as his own. It seems to become the film's own as well. Most decisive in this regard is the long scene of Garrison's summation to the jury in the trial of Clay Shaw—a scene of exposition even longer than the lecture that "X" gives to Garrison in Washington (and quite different from it in tone, as we will see). Though Garrison feels morally certain that Shaw must have been *somehow* involved in the plot to kill President Kennedy, neither he nor the viewer ever knows precisely how. The actual concrete evidence that Garrison has been able to amass against Shaw is meager at best. The criminal case is weak, as Garrison himself admits several times throughout the film (to "X," to his own assistants) and as the trial judge curtly points out to him in no uncertain terms. In his summation, Garrison hardly mentions Shaw at all, concentrating instead on various other matters, including what he himself admits is "speculation" as to exactly what happened in Dealey Plaza on November 22, 1963.

Two things in Garrison's summation are most important. First, he demonstrates—what the film has been arguing throughout—that the forensic evidence alone establishes that there must have been more than one shooter at Dealey Plaza, and hence, by definition, a conspiracy. If, as the Warren Report alleged, there was just one gunman who fired three shots, then one of the three must, as Garrison offers to demonstrate, have been the so-called "magic bullet" that performed all sorts of weird physical impossibilities, twisting and turning this way and that in order to cause seven wounds in Kennedy and Connally. Garrison has often been portrayed in the film as proud of his record as a combat veteran of the US military; and it is with this authority that he tells the jury, "Anyone who's been in combat will tell you that never in the history of gunfire has there been a bullet this ridiculous."

The debunking of the "magic bullet" hypothesis establishes that there *was* a conspiracy to kill the president. The second crucial argument in the summation concerns what "X" has called the *why* of the plot. Here Garrison adopts the theory propounded by "X" and rephrases it in his own (quite different) terms. Like "X," the district attorney maintains that Kennedy was killed by a conspiracy directed at the highest levels of the Pentagon and the CIA because of JFK's intention to scale back the warmaking powers of America's national-security state and, most specifically, to withdraw US troops from Vietnam: in effect, to preclude the Vietnam War that, at the time of the trial, was raging under Nixon's continuation of the Johnson war policy. Garrison's tone and manner are, however, almost antithetical to those of "X." "X" had delivered his lecture with the detached cynicism of one whose own involvement with Blacks Ops seems always to have been motivated less by the anti-communist zeal driving a Guy Bannister or a David Ferrie than by a skilled player's relish of the game for its own sake. Garrison, by contrast, speaks with patriotic passion. He tells the jury that it is their duty as Americans to defend their country against the government that continues to cover up the conspiracy (for instance, by refusing to serve Garrison's subpoenas of Allen Dulles and other important Washington figures of the national-security establishment). Quoting Kennedy's Inaugural Address and Lincoln's Gettysburg Address, Garrison implores the jury to ask, not what their country can do for them, but what they can do for their country: and the main thing, he says, that they can do is to defend the survival of government of, by, and for the people. He ends by telling the members of the jury that nothing in their lives will ever be more important.

Shaw, of course, is acquitted, as in real life. Also as in real life, the jury, or at least some of it, accepts that Kennedy was murdered by conspiracy but considers that Garrison failed to prove Shaw's involvement beyond all reasonable doubt: something that the film's Garrison would, indeed, find difficult to deny. As Shaw and Garrison separately exit the courtroom, the film's drama ends, and white words on a black screen inform us of a number of real-world facts: most notably, that US military involvement in Southeast Asia cost two million Asian lives, 58,000 American lives, and $220 billion. This, then, is what, according to the film, we know. John Kennedy was killed by a conspiracy, but one whose details remain frustratingly obscure, as obscure as the details surrounding the rape and the killing in *Rashomon*. Many intriguing possibilities are suggested, but no certain specific conclusions about the who and the how of the assassination can be reached: and, indeed, the high level on which the conspiracy appears to have been planned and directed crucially helps to *keep* the details obscure. It does, however, seem overwhelmingly probable that the conspiracy resulted in the massive slaughter of the Vietnam War: always the central preoccupation of Oliver Stone's filmmaking career. *JFK* is, in its own way, as much about Vietnam as is Stone's trilogy of war films (*Platoon* [1986], *Born on the Fourth of July* [1989], and *Heaven & Earth* [1993]) whose making was interspersed by the making of *JFK* (and of several other films). Not only does the film ultimately see the Vietnam War as the most important consequence of the assassination. On the way to establishing this conclusion, the film also signals the centrality of the war in many more casual ways, *en passant*—for instance, in the way that Stone's cameras frequently focus on televisions sets tuned to news reports from war-torn Vietnam. It may seem incongruous that the film is named not after its actual protagonist—Jim Garrison—but after the president who hardly even appears in it save briefly in nonfictional archival footage.[30] But the point is that JFK was the "father-leader" (as Garrison calls him in his summation to the jury) who could and would have prevented the horrors of the Vietnam War. It is now time to examine this assumption.

JFK: Father-Leader

Was Kennedy indeed the father-leader determined to set the power of his office against the military-industrial complex about which his White House predecessor had warned (a warning of which Stone's film, as we have noted, has reminded us at its beginning)? If so, then his murder—however, exactly, it may have been accomplished—was a disaster of catastrophic proportions. Garrison, in his summation to the jury, refers to perhaps the most moving tragedy ever written in order to describe the gravity of the situation: "We've all become Hamlets in our country, children of a slain father-leader whose killers still possess the throne. The ghost of John F. Kennedy confronts us with the secret murder at the heart of the American Dream." The courtroom rhetoric here analogizes Kennedy's ghost to that of old King Hamlet in Shakespeare's play, who appears, at least in the memory of his son, as the ideal patriarch and ruler, the virtually perfect father-leader. In order to understand how Stone is constructing JFK here, it is necessary to return to the history of the actual, real-life Kennedy Administration.

We have seen that a fundamental conservatism reminiscent of (and very likely inspired at least partly by) Lord Melbourne characterized Kennedy's politics in general and, in particular, his response to the most intense national moral crisis of his time, the civil rights movement. Kennedy's general approach to foreign and military policy was no exception to this generalization. Not only did JFK willingly inherit the Cold War anti-communism that had been the central obsession of US foreign policy since the Truman Administration (and with roots that extended back to the Wilson Administration): He embraced it with a special zest. A convenient way to examine JFK's foreign policy is through his Inaugural Address, by far the most famous speech he ever gave and the most famous of all presidential speeches since Franklin Roosevelt's administration. Though political rhetoric does not always correspond exactly to political action, the Inaugural is, in fact, a fairly reliable roadmap to (at least most of) the actions of the Kennedy Administration.

The speech deals far more with global than with domestic matters, and wastes little time in striking a note as confident and bellicose as the most militant Cold Warrior could have wished. Barely 90 seconds into the address, this challenge is offered:

> Let the word go forth from this time and place, to friend and foe alike, that the torch has been passed to a new generation of Americans—born in this century, tempered by war, disciplined by a hard and bitter peace, proud of our ancient heritage—and unwilling to witness or permit the slow undoing of those human rights to which this nation has always been committed, and to which we are committed today at home and around the world.

The reference to "a new generation" that was "born in this century," reminds us that Kennedy, born 27 years after Eisenhower, was the youngest man ever elected to the presidency; and "tempered by war" is a skillful allusion to the combat heroism that US Navy Lieutenant John F. Kennedy had displayed in the Pacific theatre of World War II.[31] Most important, "disciplined by a hard and bitter peace" refers directly to the Cold War, and rousingly affirms the anti-communism to which Kennedy (like his father) had always been firmly attached. The stated commitment to "human rights" has nothing to do with the deprivation of such rights by the racist white oligarchies of the American South (the civil rights movement is never even mentioned in the speech), nor is there any hint that it might refer to the tyranny of such anti-communist US allies as Franco of Spain, Chiang Kai-shek of Taiwan, or the Shah of Iran. Human rights, clearly, are to be upheld only when they are violated by the Stalinist regimes of the USSR, China, and their allies. Lest there should be any doubt of his militant Cold Warriorship, Kennedy immediately followed the period quoted above with this memorable sentence: "Let every nation know, whether it wishes us well or ill, that we shall pay any price, bear any burden, meet any hardship, support any friend, oppose any foe, in order to assure the survival and the success of liberty." Aside from the concluding admonition to "ask not what your country can do for you—ask what you can do for your country," this sentence has, in retrospect, become the most widely remembered part of the entire speech: but not, usually, in admiration. It is rather recalled as the rhetorical seed of the horrific slaughter in Vietnam—though, of course, US support was, in standard Cold War fashion, given not to the "liberty" Kennedy hymned but to the Diêm and succeeding anti-communist dictatorships of South Vietnam.[32]

Most of Kennedy's foreign and military policy reflected the personal aggressiveness and the Cold War anti-communism of the Inaugural Address. In 1961, depressed after having been wrong-footed by Khrushchev during their summit meeting in Vienna, JFK seriously contemplated launching a nuclear war over the comparatively trivial matter of a proposed treaty between the Soviet Union and East Germany that could have limited American access to West Berlin. During the Cuban Missile Crisis of 1962, Kennedy brought the world even closer to nuclear holocaust and, indeed, at some points seemed to be actively trying for war. Though the crisis was finally resolved peacefully and without an American invasion of Cuba, the restraint that saved the world was almost entirely on Khrushchev's side. Kennedy claimed to be concerned only about

Soviet missiles in Cuba. But, when Khrushchev proposed that he would withdraw those missiles in exchange for a withdrawal of American missiles from Turkey—missiles that were militarily obsolete and scheduled to be withdrawn anyway—Kennedy refused the deal.[33] The only alternative to war that he would accept was the most complete and abject surrender on Khrushchev's part (a surrender generally considered to have been largely responsible for Khrushchev's ouster by Leonid Brezhnev two years later). As to Vietnam itself, though American military involvement there had begun under Eisenhower, there were only about 900 US troops (euphemistically designated "advisers") in Vietnam when Kennedy delivered his Inaugural Address. Kennedy increased that number to over 16,000—far fewer, of course, than the half million troops that Johnson would send but nonetheless a substantial escalation of the military situation that JFK had inherited.

But JFK's ardent Cold Warriorship was not the whole story of his foreign and military policy. One might argue that, just as he generally tried to have it both ways on civil rights—attempting to please the civil rights movement and its supporters without too greatly offending the racist sensibilities of the white South—so, on global matters, he could be dovish as well as hawkish. The analogy is far from perfect. However disappointed Martin Luther King and other civil rights leaders often were by what they saw as Kennedy's lukewarm and unreliable commitment to their cause, his words and actions in support of civil rights were nonetheless considerably more forthright and more frequent than any challenges he offered to the anti-communist hawkishness that he usually upheld. But his sometime dovishness was real enough; and there is some evidence that, when it came to the Cold War, the president who was gunned down in Dallas in November 1963 was not quite the same person as the one who took the oath of office in Washington in January 1961.

Indeed, even the Inaugural Address is not completely univocal in this regard. In addition to his pugnacious challenges to the Soviet

Union, Kennedy also requested "that both sides [in the Cold War] begin anew the quest for peace, before the dark powers of destruction unleashed by science engulf all humanity in planned or accidental self-destruction." True, this dovish note was immediately followed by the hawkish guarantee, "We dare not tempt them with weakness. For only when our arms are sufficient beyond doubt can we be certain beyond doubt that they will never be employed." Yet the speech does go on to call on the USSR to agree on arms-control measures and to cooperate with the United States in scientific, technological, medical, commercial, and other endeavors. The beautifully crafted rhetoric of the Inaugural Address was mainly the work of Ted Sorensen, JFK's principal speechwriter and, later, one of his first serious biographers. But the spirit animating it was in many ways Lord Melbourne's: presumptively attached to the status quo, but not unthinkingly or inflexibly so, and with a certain balanced wariness of all absolutes.

Rhetorically, Kennedy's dovish side was most memorably and most emphatically expressed in a speech delivered more than two years after the Inaugural: his commencement address at American University in June 1963. More than half again as long as the Inaugural, the speech is almost entirely devoted to the subject of peace between the US and the USSR. Kennedy stressed both the enormous cost of the military establishments maintained by the two superpowers and the global devastation that would result if their nuclear arms were ever actually used. Very unusually for a US leader during the Cold War, he maintained that Americans as well as Soviets needed to rethink their attitudes toward one another. He pointed out that, "[a]lmost unique among the major world powers," the two nations had never fought against each other in war; and he acknowledged the enormous human and material costs that the USSR had suffered during World War II. While remaining firmly opposed to communism as "a negation of personal freedom and dignity," Kennedy nonetheless paid tribute to Soviet achievements "in science and space, in economic and industrial growth, in culture, in acts of courage." He committed the United States to the ultimate goal of "general and complete disarmament," and, in the shorter run, described the then-current negotiations that within two months would lead to the Test Ban Treaty—which, it should be emphasized, was achieved against the opposition of hawks not only in Congress but also in JFK's own State Department. In the most widely remembered part of the speech, Kennedy suggested that peace between the superpowers was a cause of such existential moment as to transcend all political divisions: "[I]n the final analysis, our most basic common link is that we all inhabit this small planet. We all breathe the same air. We all cherish our children's futures. And we are all mortal." Perhaps equally noteworthy, though much less often noted, is the fact that, even though the matter might not have seemed directly pertinent to the overall theme of world peace, the commencement address—unlike the Inaugural—does expressly mention the domestic struggle for civil rights. Kennedy declared that "peace and freedom walk together," and called upon all levels of American government and all US citizens "to respect the rights of others and respect the law of the land."

In the brief, admiring narrative of the Kennedy Administration offered by the newsreel at the beginning of *JFK*, the Inaugural Address is completely ignored, while the American University speech figures prominently. Yet—with the important exception of the Test Ban Treaty itself—one can hardly name major concrete actions by President Kennedy that reflected the spirit of the AU commencement address. It can, indeed, be hypothesized that the AU speech expressed a genuine change of heart, but one that simply came too late in JFK's violently shortened presidency to find much expression beyond the rhetorical kind. At one point in the speech, Kennedy maintained that the superpowers must avoid "confrontations which bring an adversary to a choice of either a humiliating retreat or a nuclear war": i.e., exactly the choice that he had himself forced upon Khrushchev less than a year earlier. Was this matchlessly hypocritical effrontery—or an implied self-criticism, a tacit admission that he had learned something since the previous October?[34] We can never really know.

Likewise, we can never know what the ultimate significance of National Security Action Memorandum 263 would have been if the gunmen (or, as the Warren Report would have it, gunman) at Dealey Plaza had missed their target. As we have seen, the fictional "X" in Stone's film leans heavily on NSAM 263 in formulating his theory of the assassination. Similarly, in real life, the memorandum (which "X" describes accurately enough) has indeed often been cited as crucial evidence by those who maintain that Johnson's war policy was a reversal and betrayal of Kennedy's—rather than, as others have argued, a logical continuation of Kennedy's policy and, in all probability, similar to what JFK would have done had he lived. But Kennedy made a special point of keeping the contents of NSAM 263 secret, so, though the document technically represented official national policy, it did not irrevocably commit the president to anything. Perhaps—as "X" in the film seems to assume—it did represent what he was fully determined to do, and perhaps he would have attempted to implement it despite furious opposition from the Pentagon and its allies. Or perhaps it was just one possibility that he was toying with. Perhaps, indeed, the ultimate import of NSAM 263 was never quite clear even in Kennedy's own mind. Certainly the memorandum, like the AU commencement address to which it bears an evident affinity, represents an aspect of Kennedy's thinking on foreign and military policy, an aspect that seems to have become increasingly important during the president's final months. But it is something of a leap to conclude that the speech and the memorandum prove beyond doubt that JFK had left the Cold Warriorship and the general Melbournian conservatism of his entire earlier career decisively behind.[35]

Such is the leap that *JFK* makes. In the established manner of historical fiction, Stone's film constructs Kennedy in a plausible and aesthetically satisfying way, but not one unassailable by the standards of nonfictional scholarship. The movie soft-pedals (while not completely denying) the zealous Cold Warriorship of Kennedy's earlier career, and emphatically presents him as, by the end, the ideal father-leader and an unequivocal anti-militarist hero, a determined opponent of the national-security state. In Garrison's summation to the jury, the district attorney ranks JFK alongside his brother Robert and Martin Luther King as "men whose commitment to peace and change made them dangerous to men committed to war"—though both RFK and Dr. King were actually, when they were themselves gunned down in 1968, far more explicitly opposed to the Cold War consensus (at that time being fractured by the Vietnam War) than John Kennedy had ever been. To recur to the Shakespearian analogy suggested in the Introduction to this volume, one might say that Stone gives us the best feasible version of JFK just as Shakespeare gives us the worst feasible version of Richard III. Stone gives Kennedy the benefit of every conceivable doubt and always shows him in the most favorable light, just as Shakespeare gives Richard the benefit of nothing and consistently constructs the historical record in the way least flattering to him.

It is worth recalling that, as many Shakespeare scholars have pointed out, the playwright had political as well as aesthetic reasons for painting Richard as a totally monstrous Machiavellian villain. The ultimate historical source of the play, and in particular the source of Richard's elaborate villainy in it, was Thomas More's *History of King Richard the Third*, published in 1513, when More was an important government official under Henry VIII. Henry had inherited the throne from his father, Henry VII, who had seized it, and founded the Tudor dynasty, when he defeated and killed Richard at the Battle of Bosworth Field: so that, by portraying Richard as utterly evil, More was cannily offering a tacit justification for the legitimacy of his own sovereign. Shakespeare, living and writing under Henry VII's granddaughter, Elizabeth I, had similar reasons to follow More on the matter. But it was probably not just a question of tactical prudence. We must remember that, for Shakespeare's Elizabethan audience, the civil wars of the fifteenth century were a relatively fresh—and profoundly worrying—historical memory. Indeed, Shakespeare himself mightily *refreshed* such memories with the tetralogy of plays that is concluded by *Richard III* (the first three plays of the tetralogy are the three parts of *Henry VI*). By helping to confirm the legitimacy of the Tudor dynasty, which had restored civil peace to England, Shakespeare presumably felt that he was not only strengthening his own personal position but also performing a valuable patriotic service.

Stone is clearly no less patriotic: Only, his service is not to celebrate the legitimacy of the government under which he lives but, precisely, to question and undermine it. "A patriot must always be ready to defend his country against its government," as Garrison, in his summation, quotes.[36] In this vein, *JFK* celebrates its titular character as the ideal father-leader, as America's equivalent of Shakespeare's old King Hamlet as remembered by his son the Prince, in order to suggest that the United States had—and hence, on some level, still potentially has—an alternative to the military-industrial complex against which Eisenhower warned. There is nothing inevitable, the film seems to say, about the horrors that the military-industrial complex has unleashed. Johnson, Nixon, and the functionaries of the national-security state in general—"men committed to war," in Garrison's description—have produced the insane slaughter of the Vietnam War. But their version of America is not the only one possible: and the proof is that a man resolutely opposed to what they stood for recently managed to rise to the White House itself.

It is in this context that we can best understand the unique campaign of defamation against Stone's film that the American journalistic establishment launched upon, and even somewhat before, the appearance of *JFK* in theatres. If Stone had made a film simply suggesting that the Vietnam policy Kennedy planned to pursue was wiser and more just than the policies actually implemented by Johnson and Nixon, there would almost certainly have been no particular fuss. Probably most, or at least many, journalists in 1991 would have largely agreed. Nor was Stone's offense only the film's rejection of the single-gunman theory of the Warren Report. As we have seen, on this point *JFK* is at one with what the House Select Committee on Assassinations had concluded more than ten years earlier. The far more radical move that the film makes is to question, as Garrison expressly does more than once in his summation to the jury, whether the United States is actually a functioning democracy. If a duly elected chief executive—who is nominally, in constitutional theory, the supreme commander of the entire armed apparatus of the national-security state—can be murderously dispatched by that apparatus when he is seen to be threatening its essential purposes, then America's claim to democratic governance is seriously problematic at best. Perhaps, contrary to electoral theory, the people are not really sovereign after all.

In the perspective of world history, there is, of course, nothing especially shocking in this suggestion: Kings are killed, as "X" puts it—it happens all the time. But the American journalistic establishment has never been willing to consider that the kind of power politics that is familiar (as "X" says) in all times and places to students of history is operative in its *own* country. Since the onset of the Cold War under Truman, the military-industrial complex—which, it is worth pointing out, could even be *named* only by an untouchable five-star general, and even by him only when he was on his way out of public life—has been sacrosanct for liberal as much as for conservative mainstream journalists. It is, indeed, generally permissible to question the *wisdom* of the guardians of the national-security state, to suggest that they may sometimes offer unsound advice to the civilian executive. But to maintain, as "X" and the film itself do, that such guardians may ruthlessly and murderously pursue their own material interests in defiance of elected officials is quite a few bridges too far. It is far too wounding to the American self-image that mainstream American journalism functions to protect. It is far too transgressive of the quasi-official state religion of American "exceptionalism." Most important of all, it is far too dangerous, potentially, to the national-security state. There are, to be sure, radically left-wing works of art and scholarship, with their mostly marginal audiences, that pursue the essential theses of *JFK* as militantly, or, indeed, more militantly than the film itself. But they can be safely ignored with Marcusean "repressive tolerance." On the other hand, for a "major motion picture"—a Hollywood film, a Warner Brothers film, a brilliantly entertaining work of cinema with popular stars and superstars—to show that American politics is, as "X" puts it, power and *nothing more* was, for America's political journalists, a capital offense. Like Kennedy himself as "X" tells it, the movie had to be killed.

JFK: Son-Avenger

And yet it wasn't killed. The "relative autonomy" of the cultural and, more specifically, the cinematic level proved, in this instance, sufficiently powerful to help to assure the film's success. Actually, the political journalists who tried to assassinate *JFK* were, in at least one way, in a somewhat weak position from the beginning. Despite their almost unchallenged dominance of the mainstream media, their efforts to make the lone-gunman theory sacrosanct have never been particularly successful with the public at large. With remarkable consistency, polling over the years and decades has indicated that a substantial majority of Americans are dubious of the Warren Report and inclined to believe that Kennedy was murdered by a conspiracy. Stone's film was thus able to appeal immediately to the filmgoing public over the heads of the nation's journalistic gatekeepers; and its brilliant construction as a taut, suspenseful thriller guaranteed a wide popularity.

It remains to examine the dramatic and political significance of the thriller's construction of its operative protagonist, Jim Garrison. The film is partly based on one of the actual Garrison's books,[37] and Garrison himself cooperated with the making of the film, even acting a minor role in it (ironically, that of his nemesis, Earl Warren). Nonetheless, Garrison as Stone and Costner represent him is far from a straight biographical portrayal of the New Orleans district attorney. To say so is not to accede to the numerous journalistic slanders against Garrison that often accompanied the attacks on Stone's movie. Many of the journalists hostile to *JFK* objected to the generally (though by no means completely) favorable portrayal of its central character, and charged the real-life Garrison with numerous misdeeds, such as bribing and threatening witnesses and even maintaining relations with organized crime—all allegations that nobody has ever substantiated. Garrison was, in 1973, tried in federal court for accepting bribes—a prosecution that he maintained was mere retaliation for his prosecution of Clay Shaw—but he acted as his own defense attorney and was found not guilty on all charges. After serving as DA of Orleans Parish, he was elected to a judgeship on the Louisiana Fourth Circuit Court of Appeal, a position that he held until his death from cancer the year after *JFK* was released.

Nonetheless, it is clear that *JFK* constructs a Garrison rather different from that really known to the voters of New Orleans.[38] The Louisiana—and especially the New Orleans—electorate has often displayed an attraction to colorful, flamboyant, fun-loving politicians. The Long brothers remain the most famous examples, while Edwin Edwards, the most important figure in modern Louisiana politics, made no secret of his fondness for gambling and womanizing, and was elected governor a record-breaking four times. Garrison, by all accounts, fit well into this pattern. He earned his local nickname, "the Jolly Green Giant," not only because of his height—he stood six foot six—but also for exemplifying the quasi-official motto of southern Louisiana, *Laissez les bon temps rouler!* ("Let the good times roll!").

But neither the nickname nor the motto are ever mentioned in Stone's film, which almost completely erases this side of the historical Garrison. We do see, in perhaps the closest thing to an exception which *JFK* offers, that Garrison is a regular customer at Antoine's, and that, when he arrives at the restaurant—the oldest and one of most famous and most elegant in New Orleans—he can count on a martini waiting at his table. Yet, significantly, in the pertinent scene Garrison is at Antoine's not, primarily, to have a good time, but to meet with his assistants and to work with them on the investigation of JFK's murder. Throughout the film Garrison is portrayed as consistently solemn and attentive to public duty, with Costner hardly ever even cracking a smile. In an early scene, Liz Garrison, attempting with some difficulty to arrange a Saturday-night "date" with her husband in their bedroom, even remarks, only half in jest, that her mother had warned her of the consequences if she should marry such a serious man as Jim. If the real-life Garrison had actually been as dour as Stone and Costner's representation of him, he might not have enjoyed anything like his actual record of electoral success.

The Garrison of *JFK* is constructed out of—or at least heavily influenced by—several sources besides the actual New Orleans DA. In the Shakespearian analogy suggested in the long scene of Garrison's summation to the jury, the correspondence of President Kennedy to old King Hamlet as the ideal father-leader is, as we have seen, made explicit. Though the district attorney maintains that the role of young Prince Hamlet is dispersed among the American citizenry at large—"We've all become Hamlets in our country"—it is evident, though unstated, that, if there is one particular

American who corresponds to the son determined to avenge his father's murder and the usurpation of his father's throne, it must be Garrison himself. Though in real life Garrison was only four years younger than Kennedy, in the film he has cast himself in the role of the son-avenger, determined not only to prosecute Clay Shaw but to challenge the entire military-industrial complex that he holds to be the ultimate killer of the president. The dramatic structures of *Hamlet* and *JFK* are in this way parallel—the two father-leaders have only a marginal presence on stage or screen, while the two son-avengers are the real protagonists—and the gravity of Garrison's character as constructed by Stone and Costner owes much to the (literally) deadly-serious nature of Prince Hamlet and his mission of revenge. Far from being jolly or green, Prince Hamlet famously dresses in black and maintains a demeanor that is very much the opposite of jolly.

There is another fictional character who is perhaps even more important than Prince Hamlet as a source of the film's Garrison: Atticus Finch, the most iconic representation of the virtuous Southern attorney perfectly dedicated to public duty. Owing to Harper Lee's popular and widely taught novel *To Kill a Mockingbird* (1960) and, even more, to Gregory Peck's Oscar-winning performance in Robert Mulligan's 1962 film version of the same title, the almost invariably solemn Atticus—who, in the Deep South during the Great Depression, defends a black man falsely accused of rape by a white woman—has become probably the most influential model of lawyerly virtue in US cultural history. Atticus defends, while Garrison prosecutes; and Atticus's case is of immediate interest only locally, while Garrison's involves national and international conspiracies of global importance. But the two men share an absolute, unbending, unsmiling determination to do the right thing in the face of enormous pressure to do otherwise—whether that pressure be exerted by a handful of local Ku Klux types or by the high authorities of the military-industrial complex. Doubtless more than a few real-life legal careers have been at least partly inspired by Lee's novel and Mulligan's film, and Atticus Finch has had notable fictional progeny as well—for instance, the small-town Southern district attorney Forrest Bedford (Sam Waterston) in the justly acclaimed television series *I'll Fly Away* (NBC, 1991–1993). But Stone's Garrison is perhaps the most notable of them all. *JFK* even contains an all but explicit cinematic allusion to the earlier film. Mulligan's scene in which Atticus talks reassuringly to his daughter on the typically Southern front-porch swing of their house is visually echoed by a closely similar scene in Stone's movie in which Garrison comforts two of his children on their own home's front-porch swing.

Yet another source of Stone's Garrison is not a particular fictional character like Prince Hamlet or Atticus Finch but a character type of special importance in the Stone *oeuvre*: the male innocent, or relative innocent, who begins by taking the world around him pretty much as he finds it, and who willingly conforms to the dominant ideologies of his society, but who gradually comes to see that the social structures that he has taken for granted are saturated with evil and becomes, in one way and to one degree or another, a rebel against them. Prior to *JFK*, Stone had been successful with such iterations of the type as the green soldier Chris Taylor (Charlie Sheen) in *Platoon*, the struggling young stockbroker Bud Fox (Charlie Sheen) in *Wall Street* (1987), and—perhaps most impressively— the gung-ho Marine Ron Kovic (Tom Cruise) in *Born on the Fourth of July*. Much later, Stone would return to this theme with Edward Snowden (Joseph Gordon-Levitt) in *Snowden* (2016).

The Garrison of *JFK* is not precisely similar to these other examples, since we first meet him as already older and more mature: He is, after all, not a raw recruit like Chris Taylor but the DA of Orleans Parish. Nonetheless, he corresponds pretty well to the type. Garrison, as he enters the drama of *JFK*, is happily successful both in his chosen profession and as a husband and father. Though already known as a liberal (at least by Louisiana standards), he is a fairly conventional prosecuting attorney. Soon after the assassination, he brings David Ferrie (known to his investigators as an associate of Oswald's) in for questioning; and he finds Ferrie's account of his recent movements suspicious enough that he detains him for further questioning by the FBI. But, when the FBI not only releases Ferrie at once but issues an unusual statement saying that questioning him in the first place was entirely Garrison's idea, and not theirs at all, Garrison merely says, as though with a shrug, "They must know something we don't." It is only three years later—after his fateful conversation with Senator Long and, especially, after he takes to reading all 26 volumes of the Warren Report with close attention—that Garrison decides there is more to the Kennedy assassination than anyone has yet discovered. Furthermore, it is only after his conversation with "X" that Garrison, though always an admirer of JFK, truly comes to see him as the ideal father-leader, murdered by the usurpers who control the national-security state. The solemnity of the film's Garrison is in large part the solemnity of the *convert*. His commitment is held with the special zeal of the believer who has come to his current understanding of things through a difficult and sometimes painful process of discovery that has required the abandonment of many of the assumptions that he had held as a matter of course. The rhetoric of conversion is sometimes explicit in the film. In one of the several exchanges in which Liz Garrison reproaches her husband for neglecting his family as the investigation into Kennedy's murder eats up more and more of his time and energy, she tells him that he has changed. "Of course I've changed!" he thunders back. "My eyes have opened! And, once they've opened, believe me, what used to look normal looks insane."

Though Costner-as-Garrison, like Peck-as-Atticus, manifestly shows that this kind of fiercely serious character can pack considerable dramatic punch, it is worth considering that Stone might have constructed a more immediately engaging character if he had stuck closer to the real-life New Orleans DA. Certainly the cine-matic possibilities of the Jolly Green Giant, the big convivial man happily at home in the bars and restaurants of his city's sybaritic French Quarter, must have occurred to him. But Stone's transfor-mation of his lead character into a deeply solemn crusader in the manner of Atticus Finch—and, unlike Atticus, a crusader with the special fervor of the convert—is important for the ultimate politi-cal thrust of the movie.

Garrison, as we have seen, knows that the legal case against Clay Shaw is flimsy, and, indeed, at one point comments that it is only by beating the long odds against them that his team can possibly win a criminal conviction. Deprived of the opportunity to ques-tion Allen Dulles and his top associates under penalty of perjury, Garrison has relatively little hope of proving beyond all reason-able doubt that Shaw ever worked for the CIA, still less that he was directly involved in Kennedy's murder. (But after the close of the film proper, we are informed that, as a matter of fact, ten years after the Shaw trial Richard Helms, who in 1963 had been the CIA's Director of Covert Operations, testified under oath that Shaw had indeed been employed by the Agency.) In this way, the Shaw prosecution is fundamentally flawed from the start, since a district attorney is normally expected to bring to court only those cases in which there is fair probability that guilt can be proved beyond reasonable doubt.

For Garrison, however, and for *JFK*, this point of appropriate prosecutorial conduct is massively outweighed by the patriotic—and metaphorically filial—duty to expose and avenge the assassi-nation of President Kennedy. For Garrison—and it is here that his construction by Stone and Costner as an uncompromisingly solemn and determined crusader is especially crucial—the Shaw trial is but the first stage of a campaign that he expects to last his entire lifetime or longer. "If it takes me 30 years to nail every one of these assassins, then I will continue this investigation for 30 years," as he says to reporters while leaving the courtroom immediately after the Shaw acquittal. Earlier, in his summation to the jury, Garrison has suggested an even longer time-scale. He notes that the Johnson and then the Nixon White House have ordered that 51 CIA documents pertaining to Lee Oswald and Jack Ruby be kept under seal for 75 years. He goes on to say,

> I'm in my early 40s, so I'll have shuffled off this mortal coil by then. [That Garrison should allude to his own death with a quotation from his fellow son-avenger Prince Hamlet's most famous soliloquy is of course significant.] But I'm already telling my eight-year-old son to keep himself physically fit, so that, one glorious September morning in the year 2038, he can walk into the National Archives and find out what the CIA and the FBI knew. They may even push it back then. Hell, it may become a generational affair, with questions passed down from father to son, mother to daughter. But someday, somewhere, someone may find out the damn truth. We better. We better, or we might just as well build ourselves another government, like the Declaration of Independence says to, when the old one ain't working—just a little farther out west.

Contrary to what some who have willfully misunderstood Stone's movie have assumed, the Garrison of *JFK* is under no illusion that a single trial or a single revelation could suddenly render the entire system of the military-industrial complex transparent and vulnerable. The struggle that he envisions against the national-security state is a multi-decadal, perhaps a multi-generational, affair, with the Shaw prosecution only the opening skirmish in a long war. It is a war whose necessary telos may be nothing less than revolution itself, a revolution whose fundamental justification can be found in the American Revolution of 1776 and the Jeffersonian *apologia* for it in the Declaration of Independence. As we have seen, Garrison, in his summation, quotes the maxim that a patriot must always be ready to defend his country against its government: and that, of course, was precisely what Jefferson, Washington, Franklin, and the other Founders did.

It is important to recognize—yet another point frequently overlooked by the film's detractors—that the Garrison of *JFK*, while a deeply admirable and sympathetic character, is not a flawless one (in this way he is more like Prince Hamlet than like Atticus Finch). Liz Garrison has a real point with her complaints that Jim seems unconcerned about the extent to which the Kennedy investigation is driving him to shirk his family responsibilities: "I think you care more about John Kennedy than your own family," as she once says. (Here the contrast with Atticus, the perfect though single father, is particularly sharp.) Even within his professional capacity, Garrison is represented as having plenty of faults. He can be short-tempered, short-sighted, arbitrary, and inept in the running of the investigation and the management of his subordinates. Perhaps the most notable example is his firing of his utterly loyal top investigator Lou Ivon (Jay O. Sanders) when Lou tries to explain to him—quite accurately— that the assistant district attorney Bill Broussard is treacherous (Bill, after being threatened by a local FBI agent, has been secretly passing confidential material to the federal authorities).

Yet, flawed human being though Jim Garrison may be, the film is completely and most consequentially at one with him in his earnest determination—single-minded, and sometimes literally sleepless— to pursue the struggle for American democracy and against the national-security state at all costs, for as long as it takes. Garrison's reference in his summation to his young son is echoed in Stone's dedication of the film itself, "to the young in whose spirit the search for truth marches on"; and it is not accidental that Garrison's son is played by Stone's own. Aside from a few basic facts that have been unquestioned from the start—mainly those revealed by the Zapruder film—*JFK* leaves nearly all the details of the Kennedy assassination as shrouded in *Rashomon*-like mystery as it found them. There is as much enigma in the character of the assassination as in the character of Charles Foster Kane. Yet the movie, like Garrison, does nonetheless insist that the assassination provides a brief, cloudy, yet indispensable window on the unacknowledged ways that the military-industrial complex works in the United States; and it is the awesome, untouchable power of the top commanders of the national-security state that manages to keep the details of such conspiracies as the Kennedy murder mostly under wraps. In the manner of all historical fiction, *JFK* shapes both its actual hero and its titular one for its own thematic and dramatic purposes. As we have seen, the historical John Kennedy, with his frequent Melbournian detachment and conservatism, was an imperfect figure to be reconstructed as the ideal father-leader and convinced opponent of his country's secret and permanent government. Yet the historical record can rationally be read to indicate that JFK, though imperfect, was not a wholly inadequate or inappropriate vehicle for the project of *JFK*. Historians will doubtless continue to argue about what JFK "would have" done about Vietnam if the gunfire of Dealey Plaza had missed him. Meanwhile, *JFK* invites us to consider the forces in the American polity that have made the Vietnam War—and much other mass killing—possible.

CHAPTER II
Nixon: Tragic Hero-Villain

Nixon: Tragic Hero-Villain

From Kennedy to Nixon

In order to understand the structure of the duology composed of *JFK* (1991) and *Nixon* (1995), it is useful to begin by examining the juxta-position of the two men that is presented by the historical record. It is probably fair to say that, at least since 1974—when Nixon became the only American president ever forced to resign his office in disgrace— the dominant (though certainly not universal) impression of the duo has been of Kennedy as a shining Sir Galahad and of Nixon as his polar opposite, an unprincipled and treacherous villain like Galahad's antitype, Mordred. During his time in office, JFK's average approval rating was a stunning 70.1 percent, easily the highest of any US presi-dent since World War II. (Eisenhower ranks second with 65 percent). Though JFK's rating somewhat declined late in his truncated term, it was still a more than healthy 58 percent by the end. In Stone's film, Nixon (Anthony Hopkins) is quite reasonably portrayed as having no interest in staging a rematch with Kennedy in the 1964 presidential election, so convinced is Nixon that Kennedy will be unbeatable. Furthermore, as popular as Kennedy was while alive and in office, the halo of martyrdom conferred by the assassination has given him, in retrospect, an air of heroic saintliness unlike that enjoyed by any other president since Lincoln.

Nixon, by contrast, left office with an abysmal 24 percent approval rating, less than half of his unimpressive presidential average of 49 percent. Even long before the burglary of the offices of the Democratic National Committee at the Watergate complex in Washington on June 17, 1972, Nixon had always been, for many, the deceitful and badly shaven thug of the Herblock editorial cartoons. Since the Watergate scandal, he has never—now more than two generations since his departure from the White House and more than one generation since his death—really shaken off the aura of criminality.

But there is more to the story of Kennedy and Nixon than the stark opposition between Galahad and Mordred. We might begin by taking a tip from a late comment by Nixon himself. During the last four years of his life, Nixon adopted as his final protégé—and, it seems, as a kind of granddaughter figure—the young right-wing political writer Monica Crowley. She spent many hours talking and (mainly) listening to Nixon on various matters of politics, government, and world affairs; and, after his death, she published two books that were based on these conversations. In one, she records him saying, "The 1960 election was probably the greatest election of this century because the candidates were both outstanding."[39] Though obviously self-serving, in the characteristic Nixon way, this remark may be useful in reminding us how brilliantly successful the two careers were (in Nixon's case, until his self-destruction in Watergate) and how the two men once had more in common than is usually remembered.

Both US Navy veterans of the Pacific theatre of World War II, Kennedy (only 29) and Nixon (only 33) were elected to the US House of Representatives the year after the war ended, in 1946. Partly owing to the accident that they were assigned offices near one another, the two young men quickly became personal friends, despite being of opposed parties ("We came to Congress together, we were like brothers," says Stone's Nixon of himself and JFK). In the recent election, JFK had enjoyed the advantage of being both the son of an immensely wealthy banker, who lavishly financed his son's campaign, and the grandson of a major Boston politician, his namesake, former Mayor John Fitzgerald (who was popularly known as "Honey Fitz"); and he thus had a fairly easy time winning an open seat in an overwhelmingly Democratic district. But he was re-elected twice and then, in 1952, performed the genuinely impressive feat of running for the Senate and defeating Henry Cabot Lodge, the three-term Republican incumbent and the scion of what had been, until that point, the most politically powerful family in modern Massachusetts history: and this despite the fact that, simultaneously in the presidential election, Eisenhower was winning a landslide victory for the Republicans both nationally and in Massachusetts.

In 1956, Kennedy, still not yet 40, emerged as a fully national figure, narrowly losing the vice-presidential nomination at the Democratic Convention to the much more experienced and better known Senator Estes Kefauver. In 1960, he put together a highly innovative presidential campaign that would become a model for many future campaigns (as would Nixon's 1968 campaign), and handily won the Democratic presidential nomination on the first ballot. It has been generally forgotten how huge an obstacle he had to overcome on the religious issue. Only once before, in 1928, had a major party dared to nominate a Roman Catholic for president; and that experiment ended in disaster for the Democrats. Facing such slogans as "Hoover and America, or Smith and Rome—The Choice Is Yours," New York Governor Al Smith lost to Herbert Hoover by a landslide in both the popular and electoral votes, losing not only his home state but even several states of the Old Confederacy that had never voted Republican since Reconstruction. The party was deeply traumatized by the experience, and, with anti-Catholic bigotry still widespread in 1960 in many Southern states that were indispensable for a Democratic victory, it required a campaign of unusual brilliance to persuade the Democrats to take another chance on a Catholic.

Nixon's rise was even more meteoric. With no family money or political connections behind him, and almost unknown except to his personal acquaintances, Nixon in 1946 nonetheless managed to defeat, by a wide margin, a popular and apparently well-entrenched incumbent in a California district generally supposed to be completely safe for the Democrats. He did so by running a skillful and ferocious Red-baiting campaign against Congressman Jerry Voorhis at a time when Cold War anti-communism was becoming the most effective and emotionally powerful issue in US electoral politics. Once he was in office, anti-communism continued to be Nixon's signature issue. He became a nationally prominent figure when, as a member of the House Un-American Activities Committee, he led an investigation into the alleged communist ties of the New Deal official Alger Hiss, an investigation that led to Hiss's disgrace, criminal conviction (for perjury), and imprisonment. Nixon's popularity soared. In 1948, he ran unopposed for re-election to the House. In 1950, he won an open Senate seat by a landslide, mounting another bellicose Red-baiting campaign, this time against Congresswoman Helen Gahagan Douglas, whom he dubbed "the Pink Lady." A former stage and screen actress, the physically gorgeous Douglas was, in one of Nixon's more memorable (and prurient) rhetorical flourishes, "pink right down to her underwear" (a line used verbatim in the Stone film). In an era when anti-communism dominated American politics more triumphantly than it ever did before or ever has since, Nixon managed to identify himself with the issue more prominently than anyone else did, save only Senator Joe McCarthy and FBI Director J. Edgar Hoover—both of them (sometimes) important allies of Nixon's.

Nixon's anti-communist zeal led many to associate him with the right wing of the Republican Party. This association, indeed, was one important reason that he was picked in 1952 to be General

Eisenhower's vice-presidential running mate. Eisenhower's support in the party came mainly from comparatively moderate Republicans, and Ike won the presidential nomination by defeating the right wing's number-one hero, Senator Robert Taft: so it was reasonably thought that adding Nixon to the ticket gave it some needed "balance." Nixon himself, however, always avoided identifying himself unambiguously *either* with the somewhat moderate and mainly Northeastern wing of the party *or* with the hard-right wing anchored in the Midwest and in his native California. Even while the pre-eminent Red-baiter in the House and then (along with McCarthy) in the Senate, Nixon was more moderate on certain other issues. For instance, he strongly supported foreign aid and the Marshall Plan, and he maintained a pretty consistently liberal stance on civil rights. Furthermore, during the eight years of his vice-presidency—when he managed to establish himself, in the public mind, as a real partner of the president's in a way that no earlier vice-president had ever done—Nixon was necessarily tied to what Ike upheld as "modern Republicanism." Though deliberately vague, this phrase essentially meant acceptance of existing New Deal programs, combined with opposition to further expansion of Rooseveltian reform—as opposed to the rollback of the New Deal advocated by the Taft Republicans. By 1960, Taft and McCarthy were both dead, and Eisenhower was nearing the end of his public career. Nixon was only 47 and in command of the Republican Party as nobody who was not an incumbent president had ever been before. Unlike JFK, who had to overcome fairly serious campaigns for the Democratic nomination by Hubert Humphrey, Lyndon Johnson, and others, Nixon won his party's presidential nomination against only the most token opposition.

So, as the elderly Nixon's comment to Monica Crowley suggests, the two 1960 nominees for the White House did indeed have outstanding records of political success behind them. Both had taken only fourteen years to go from being returned war veterans with no political experience to being the only two serious contenders for the most powerful office in the world. And both had achieved this triumph remarkably early in life. Though it was Kennedy, at 43, who was most often noted for youthfulness, both at the time and ever since, Nixon was, after all, only four years older. In many foreign nations, there was widespread astonishment in 1960 that the world's dominant superpower should be choosing its paramount leader from between two such youngsters. By way of comparison, in 1960 Chinese Premier Zhou Enlai was 62, Soviet Premier Nikita Khrushchev was 66, British Prime Minister Harold Macmillan was also 66, French President Charles de Gaulle was 70, Indian Prime Minister Jawaharlal Nehru was 71, and West German Chancellor Konrad Adenauer was 84.

Nor—contrary to what the Galahad/Mordred opposition would lead one to assume—were youth, early success, and a history of personal friendship the only things that Kennedy and Nixon had in common in 1960. Even on the matter on which Nixon was most extreme—Cold War anti-communism—the similarities between the two men were more striking than any differences. As we have discussed in the preceding chapter, Kennedy, at least until the final few months of his life, was a fervently anti-communist Cold Warrior. If certainly less prominent than Nixon in the ranks of anti-communism, JFK was no less committed on the issue. Perhaps most striking in this regard, it was Kennedy's sympathy for Nixon's anti-communist belligerence that led him, in 1950, to cross party lines and personally hand Nixon a $1000 campaign contribution to use in his battle against Helen Gahagan Douglas:[40] the fiercest of all of Nixon's Red-baiting operations, in which he acquired the hated nickname that followed him for the rest of his career, Tricky Dick.

As to the 1960 race itself, Nixon, looking back on it from old age, commented, "What most people forget is that Kennedy and I were a lot closer on the foreign policy issues than probably any other candidates this century."[41] This remark, which must seem shocking to those who uncritically accept the notion of Kennedy-as-Galahad, is actually something of an understatement. Though the aged Nixon was quite correct that the two candidates of 1960 were close on foreign policy and the Cold War, he could have gone on to point out that, to the extent that significant differences between them *were* expressed during the campaign, it was he himself who (usually) appeared the more moderate of the two, and Kennedy the more militant Cold Warrior. JFK invented an entirely nonexistent "missile gap," charging that the Eisenhower-Nixon Administration, though led by a five-star general, had allowed the nation's fighting strength to fall behind that of the Soviet Union. Nixon naturally defended the administration's record and maintained that there was no cause for alarm. Kennedy also blasted Ike and Dick for supposedly doing little or nothing to overthrow Fidel Castro's revolutionary government in Cuba. Nixon—who was not only familiar with the administration's secret plans to murder Castro and destroy his regime, but had probably been instrumental in organizing the operation—was moved to warn against Kennedy as a dangerous warmonger.

On the most urgent domestic issue facing the United States in 1960—the civil rights movement—Kennedy and Nixon were, again, far from reprising the roles of Galahad and Mordred, respectively. Nixon was raised, particularly by his mother, in a strongly Quaker tradition, and he was taught to revere the anti-slavery and anti-racist principles of the family's religious forerunners (like the Abolitionist poet John Greenleaf Whittier, after whom the Nixons' home town was named). When Nixon attended law school at Duke University in Durham, North Carolina, some of his Southern classmates were shocked and horrified to hear that he had eaten meals at the same table with blacks. Nixon's politics through the 1950s were fairly consistent with this background. Perhaps most notable in this connection was his extensive work with Martin Luther King to help pass the Civil Rights Act of 1957. Dr. King, though seldom

inclined to flatter or overestimate electoral politicians, was sufficiently moved by Nixon's commitment on the issue that he wrote
the vice-president a letter in which he praised Nixon's "assiduous
labor and dauntless courage," and described Nixon's work on the bill
as "certainly an expression of your devotion to the highest mandates
of the moral law."[42]

King composed no such letters to Kennedy during the 1950s.
While civil rights had become a major cause for some non-Southern
Democrats, Senator Kennedy was never among them. Instead, he
hedged and trimmed on the issue in a way that prefigured what we
have discussed in the previous chapter as his zig-zagging and flip-
flopping in the White House. When Nixon, acting in his capacity
as vice-president and hence president of the Senate, made a proce-
dural decision designed to facilitate passage of the Civil Rights Act,
Kennedy voted to overturn Nixon's ruling. Later, Kennedy voted to
weaken, arguably to the point of meaninglessness, the Act's protection of voting rights—though he did ultimately vote for the bill in
its final form. It should be recalled that, in the 1950s, the segregationist Southern bloc exercised enormous power within the Senate
Democratic caucus: so that a non-Southern Democrat always had a
strong motivation to appease the Southerners. It required real courage for any Democrat to defy the Southerners in his own caucus
(as Hubert Humphrey did) and support civil rights unequivocally
and emphatically. Kennedy, who had demonstrated unquestionable
physical bravery as a combat sailor, displayed no comparable moral
or political courage in the Senate.

Nor, ironically, did he show courage like Humphrey's in the
composition of his Pulitzer Prize-winning book *Profiles in Courage*,
published the year before the Civil Rights Act of 1957 was passed.
As in some of his Senate maneuvering, here also JFK seems to go
out of his way to mollify and even flatter the Southerners on the
matter of race and civil rights: for instance, in his elaborate praise
of the Senate acquittal of the impeached Southern racist president

Andrew Johnson, or in his repeated derision of Reconstruction and the Reconstruction politicians who supported rights for African Americans.[43] It was probably civil rights, her own signature issue, of which Eleanor Roosevelt was mainly thinking if and when (as was widely reported) she said, "I wish Kennedy had less profile and more courage."

Of course, JFK's phone call to Mrs. Martin Luther King in October 1960 changed everything. It was not only a turning point for the presidential campaign but, in retrospect, can be seen as the pivotal event (insofar as any punctiform occurrence can be so designated) that began the reconfiguration of the two parties on the race issue and ultimately led to the situation we know today, when the GOP is all but openly the party of white privilege and the Democrats command a near-unanimity of African-American support. Still, we should remember that the King family contacted the Kennedy campaign *second*, and almost as an afterthought. When the Kings first scrambled to try to save Dr. King's life, it seemed clear to them—and not unreasonably so—that, if there was any national political figure likely to help, it was Nixon.

There is, to be sure, no question but that, if we leave aside civil rights and Cold War anti-communism—two gigantic exceptions indeed—JFK did, in 1960, campaign as the more liberal of the two candidates. The gap between his relatively tepid New Dealism and Nixon's Eisenhower-style "modern Republicanism" was considerably less wide than the Grand Canyon but real enough. It is instructive to compare the candidates' respective stances toward those issues on which, as we discussed in the preceding chapter, Kennedy made his most radical proposals. Whereas Kennedy, prefiguring Medicare, argued for federal medical insurance for the elderly, Nixon (prefiguring Obamacare) maintained that the same goals could be better achieved through government support of private insurance. While Kennedy supported direct federal aid to the nation's public schools, Nixon wanted to limit Washington's involvement to providing construction loans to the individual states. Where Kennedy proposed building two million new units of public housing annually, Nixon agreed that more public housing was needed but declined to say exactly how much more. It is significant, however, that, on these issues, the differences between the candidates reflected the long-term, institutionalized commitments of their respective parties: something that was not true of civil rights or anti-communism, issues on which the two parties, at that time, did not have such clearly opposed positions, and therefore issues on which the candidates were much freer to follow their individual inclinations.[44]

In November 1960, no one could have known that Kennedy's career—and life—had only three more years to run. As we have seen, his shortened presidency was dominated for the most part by his Cold Warriorship and his general Melbournian conservatism, though it is plausibly arguable that in his final months—the months of the Test Ban Treaty, of the American University commencement address, and of National Security Action Memorandum 263—Kennedy made a sharp left turn and determined to liquidate the Cold War of which he had always been a staunch partisan. Such, of course, is the presupposition that underlies Stone's *JFK*. By contrast, 1960 was only the middle point of Nixon's political life: fourteen years after his first election to the House and fourteen years before his forced resignation of the presidency. If Kennedy arguably went on to diverge from his general stance of 1960, there is not the slightest doubt that Nixon did.

Most important here is the race issue. Through the 1950s, and into 1960, Nixon believed that the South would remain reliably Democratic for the foreseeable future and that the GOP might improve its position in some of the big, electoral-vote-rich states of the Northeast and the northern Midwest by more robustly courting the black electorate: which, though ancestrally attached to the party of Lincoln, had become increasingly Democratic since Franklin

Roosevelt and the New Deal. Events proved Nixon dead wrong, and he was quick to see it. As Lyndon Johnson championed the successful campaign to pass the Civil Rights Act of 1964—which was followed by the even more radical Voting Rights Act of 1965—it became clear that the Democratic Party was finally willing to abandon its Southern segregationist wing and declare unequivocally for civil rights to a degree that John Kennedy had never done. In the 1964 presidential contest, Barry Goldwater (who, like Nixon, had a personal history of being favorably disposed toward civil rights) rallied the white racist vote and performed the extraordinary feat (unprecedented for a Republican) of carrying five Deep South states—even while losing every other state in the union except his native Arizona.

Goldwater's own presidential hopes were irrevocably shattered by his landslide defeat. But Nixon—before almost anyone else— saw the coming realignment in US politics presaged by Goldwater's capture of states like Mississippi, Alabama, and Georgia, all hitherto completely out of reach for the Republicans. Between 1964 and 1968, furthermore, the United States was rocked by a series of highly destructive urban race riots, climaxing with those that immediately followed the assassination of Martin Luther King in April 1968. The image of African Americans as a mad, violent, dangerous horde—seldom far below the surface of the white American consciousness, and often an important factor in US electoral politics since at least the 1840s—was spectacularly revived. The 1964 vote had made clear that white "backlash" against the civil rights movement was a potent social and political force, one most concentrated in the states of the Old Confederacy though by no means unknown north of the Mason-Dixon line. Four years later, white racism had *increased* in both extent and intensity, and was looking to be a more consequential electoral factor in 1968 than at any time, probably, since the end of Reconstruction.

Nixon played on the issue with the same demagogic skill with which he had used anti-communism in the 1940s and early 1950s. Making "law and order"—the most universally understood code term of the year to appeal to white racist sensibilities—the central rallying cry of his campaign, Nixon was quite successful in building on Goldwater's Southern triumphs of four years earlier. Even though he had to compete for racist votes with the third-party candidacy of the arch-segregationist Governor George Wallace of Alabama—who carried five states in the Deep South—Nixon carried *every* other state of the Old Confederacy (except Texas, where Lyndon Johnson's political machine was still, though just barely, strong enough to win the state for Humphrey). The Democrats' Solid South, which had been indispensable to John Kennedy's victory in 1960, and which was only partly dismantled in 1964, had now been wiped from the map (though it would be fleetingly rebuilt by Jimmy Carter in 1976 just prior to vanishing forever). And the party of Lincoln was now permanently committed to white supremacy. More than any other single individual, Nixon was responsible for that elemental structural change.

On foreign policy, the differences between the Nixon of 1960 and the Nixon of 1968 and later were less dramatic. In the 1968 campaign, Nixon distanced himself from the Johnson war policy while also making clear his contempt for the antiwar movement. He discussed the Vietnam War as little as possible, and implied (though while never actually stating, contrary to what many people believe they remember) that he had a secret plan of his own to end it. Once in the White House, he spent four years prosecuting the war with a ferocity that exceeded even Johnson's, before finally withdrawing US troops. At the same time, he managed to improve relations with the Soviet Union and to open relations with China, using his history of ferocious Cold War anti-communism as a protective shield against the right-wingers too stupid to see that his (and Henry Kissinger's) long-range scheme was to construct a tacit anti-Soviet alliance between Washington and Beijing.

The dramatic "arc" of Nixon's ideological career is, then, rather more complicated than the arc of Kennedy's. With JFK, we have, from 1946 until at least 1962, a pretty consistent pattern of Cold War anti-communism, very moderate New Dealism, and general Melbournian prudence: but a pattern which is—arguably— ruptured in 1963 by a turn against the Cold War that, had Kennedy lived to follow through on it, might have amounted (as Oliver Stone asks us to believe) to a kind of humane radicalism virtually unparalleled in US history. Nixon was always more eclectic. "Tricky Dick" combined contrasting or even somewhat contradictory ideological elements that, as time went by, could be discarded, added to, made more or less prominent, or even completely reversed—all according to the changing political exigencies of the moment. Thus, the young Nixon Red-baits with a right-wing viciousness barely surpassed by Joe McCarthy himself, while also winning praise from Martin Luther King for his liberal work on civil rights. The mature Nixon, building on the sensational but transient political eruptions associated with Goldwater and Wallace, establishes white racism as the ideological glue permanently binding together the GOP; and he presides over a degree of slaughter in Vietnam beyond even what Lyndon Johnson could stomach. At the same time, he sits down for a friendly *rapprochement* with Mao Zedong—who led the most consequential communist revolution since World War II—and sees to the final significant expansion of America's welfare state until the administration of Barack Obama. Kennedy and Nixon were indeed both "outstanding," as the aged Nixon said; but it seems fair to conclude that Nixon was the more complex of the two.

The history of the two men—summarized briefly above, and, insofar as Kennedy is concerned, in the preceding chapter— constitutes, on one level, the "raw material" transmuted into works of historical fiction in *JFK* and *Nixon*.[45] But there is another, quite different kind of raw material also to be considered, namely the very different sets of generic conventions that Stone uses to shape his materials in the two films. To this matter we will now turn.

From Melodrama to Tragedy

JFK, as we considered in the preceding chapter, is an exciting and tautly constructed thriller, and, more specifically, a conspiracy thriller. Though the exact nature and extent of the conspiracy remains shrouded in *Rashomon*-like uncertainty, this epistemological indeterminacy is counterpointed by a secure *ethical* clarity. For all the things in *JFK* that are never clearly settled, what *is* firmly resolved within the fictionality of the film is the moral dichotomy between the pole of good (basically Kennedy, at least Kennedy as he had become by November 1963) and evil (the shadowy forces arrayed against him and somehow responsible for his death). Like many—probably most—thrillers, *JFK* is largely structured according to the generic conventions of melodrama.

Melodrama is often considered a simplistic form of fiction. In a *bon mot* widely attributed to Bernard Shaw, melodrama is about the conflict between right and wrong, whereas drama—that is, true drama, or drama proper—is about the conflict between right and right. But T. S. Eliot, who had a keen taste for the work of the Victorian melodramatic novelist Wilkie Collins, objected that the generic situation is more complicated than that. In contrast (and perhaps deliberate riposte) to the Shavian maxim, Eliot writes, "You cannot define Drama and Melodrama so that they shall be reciprocally exclusive; great drama has something melodramatic in it, and the best melodrama partakes of the greatness of drama." Indeed, he goes so far as to maintain that, "perhaps no drama has ever been greatly and permanently successful without a large melodramatic element." [46] It is easy to think of many and various dramas universally agreed to be great, from *Oedipus the King*, to *Hamlet*, to

Moliere's *Tartuffe*, to the four operas of Wagner's *Ring*, that illustrate Eliot's generalization. Some of Shaw's own plays could also be cited in this connection.[47]

JFK also exemplifies Eliot's point. The strictly dramatic element of the film—in the Shavian sense that drama is understood as the conflict between competing versions of right—is located mainly in the more problematic aspects of the fundamentally admirable character of the protagonist, Jim Garrison. For example, when Garrison forces the resignation of the faithful and valuable investigator Lou Ivon by refusing to fire the treacherous attorney Bill Broussard, he enacts a conflict between loyalty to his staff and a desire to foreclose internal squabbles, on the one hand, and, on the other, a clear-sighted honest judgment about how to conduct a proper investigation under already hellishly difficult circumstances. A perhaps even more noteworthy example is found in Garrison's repeated neglect of his wife and five children as the investigation of the Kennedy assassination and the prosecution of Clay Shaw take up more and more of his time. Here, indeed, we find a particular kind of tension that has resonated in Western drama for centuries, going back at least as far as the clash between the family duties and the civic duties of Sophocles's Antigone.

But this "dramatic" component of *JFK* is embedded in, and dominated by, the thoroughly and brilliantly melodramatic narrative that is decisive for the film's generic structure. As in much melodrama—think of Wilkie Collins's *The Woman in White* (1860) and *The Moonstone* (1868), or, for that matter, Dickens's *Bleak House* (1853) and *Great Expectations* (1861)—the suspense operates in two temporal directions at once. We want to discover what will happen in the future, but this discovery is inextricably bound up with uncovering buried secrets of the past. The extreme narrative skill of the movie's construction is reflected in the way that a high level of suspense is maintained even though—in contrast to the situation with most melodrama—what will happen, is, owing to the real-life historical record, known in advance by every viewer (Clay Shaw will be indicted for the Kennedy assassination and then acquitted), and the secrets of the past are revealed only in a limited and tentative way (though we have some idea of why Kennedy was killed, we never learn the identity of those, other than Shaw, who perpetrated the murder plot). As in all melodrama, the central conflict of the narrative is structured by a nearly absolute moral dichotomy. The pole of evil is in some ways made to seem all the more frighteningly wicked by being dispersed throughout an obscure conspiracy that the viewer glimpses in only the most fleeting and uncertain ways, rather than concentrated in a single and clearly present malevolent villain. Conversely, the pole of good is maintained in iconic purity by the fact that the film's titular character never really enters its dramatic action. JFK is not portrayed by an actor to any significant degree, and he is seen only briefly and almost entirely in nonfictional archival footage: There is thus no occasion to examine any of his inner moral complexities or conundrums. By replacing Kennedy himself, as the actual protagonist of the film, with the more morally complex and thus more "dramatic" character of Garrison, Kennedy's symbolic son, Stone preserves the central melodramatic moral narrative of the film—the story of the good Kennedy versus the evil conspiracy—in unassailable dominance within the overdetermined generic structure of the film. Eliot's observation about the abiding popularity of melodrama ("[M]elodrama is perennial and . . . the craving for it is perennial" [460]) helps to explain the great success of JFK at the box office, despite the almost unanimous campaign by the nation's political journalists to destroy the film.

Though Nixon certainly contains an element of melodrama, its own generic structure is dominated by a different kind of narrative: tragedy. Tragedy frequently (though not invariably) focuses on the character of a single individual. Whereas much of the interest of the conspiracy melodrama in JFK is distributed among a huge set of dramatis personae (it is worth recalling again the more than

200 speaking parts that the film boasts), *Nixon* offers an intensive psychological focus on its titular character, whose life and political career it traces in considerable detail. Appropriately, Anthony Hopkins's portrayal of the thirty-seventh president is arguably the finest single performance by any actor in the entirety of the Oliver Stone *oeuvre*. In order to understand Stone's Nixon—and Stone's *Nixon*—some consideration of the generic tragic hero is as necessary as our consideration above of the actual thirty-seventh president.

The first, most famous, and perhaps still the most useful discussion of the tragic protagonist is found in the thirteenth chapter of Aristotle's *Poetics*. The tragic hero, says Aristotle, is neither simply virtuous nor simply vicious. That a good and blameless man should be brought low by forces for which he is in no way responsible— like Stone's Kennedy destroyed by the evil scheming of the secret government—is indeed shocking, but it is, as it were, *merely* shocking. It lacks the moral complexity that, for Aristotle, inheres in the essence of tragic drama. Even less proper to tragedy is the exact opposite, the pure villain who, in being destroyed, gets exactly what he deserves. The latter kind of narrative merely satisfies our moral sense, while the former, contrasting kind merely outrages it: and the relation between morality and tragedy is, according to Aristotle, more complexly fraught than that. Tragedy is instead to be found in the downfall of "a man who is not eminently good and just, yet whose misfortune is brought about not by vice or depravity, but by some error or frailty." It is the destruction of "a man like ourselves"—a "character between these two extremes" of good and evil—that is most apt to arouse the emotions of pity and fear that Aristotle defines as the truly tragic effect.[48] The tragic hero is neither totally responsible for, nor totally innocent of, his (or, much more rarely, her) downfall.

The moral complexity of the tragic hero, then, determines the complexity of the nexus between character and fate. That there *is* such a nexus is vital. A disaster that, by mere chance, just happens to befall someone is in no way tragic. This point needs to be stressed because of the common colloquial usage in which the term and concept of tragedy are not only employed to designate events in real life (rather than on the stage, the screen, or the page) but are also made to refer to nothing but an extremely sad turn of events: as when a journalist might call the death of a family in a random car crash a "tragedy." But a pure accident cannot be tragic, because— by definition—an accident lacks the meaningfulness inherent in a genuinely tragic catastrophe. Yet, at the same time, the meaning of tragic fate cannot be too simple and straightforward. The tragic protagonist is not the victim of "poetic justice"—as when a villain is killed by the deadly trap he has set for another—nor, indeed, of any justice at all, save perhaps the roughest and most problematic sort.

If, then, the tragic hero is, as Aristotle says, a man or woman between the extremes of good and evil, Shakespearian tragedy— which in many ways illustrates Aristotle's theories even better than the Athenian tragedy with which he was himself familiar—suggests that the tragic protagonist's exact place on the moral spectrum may be both ambiguous and highly variable. Is Othello, basically, a good man and even a loving husband, who is innocently tricked into strangling Desdemona by lies of almost inconceivable malevolence? Perhaps. But one might question what kind of man not only kills his wife for presumed infidelity but does so while lacking a single piece of direct evidence (save the very ambiguous handkerchief) and possessing even indirect evidence from only a single source. King Lear is grossly irresponsible in thinking that he can renounce the duties of his royal position while maintaining its privileges and, even more, in setting up the idiotic competition among his daughters near the beginning of Act I. But that does not mean that he even remotely deserves his terrible fate, which is unforgettably and unbearably emblematized (in many productions) as he carries the body of the lifeless Cordelia just prior to his own death.

Hamlet has his faults but has usually been regarded as a mostly sympathetic character. By contrast, Macbeth must be deeply evil to allow personal ambition and a nagging wife to impel him to the treasonous murder of a friend and benefactor; but few viewers or readers have seen him as simply a villainous Elizabethan "Machiavel" like the less complexly or genuinely tragic figure of Richard III. The generic protocols of the tragic hero—while thus extremely variable—massively overdetermine the character of Stone's Nixon and, indeed, point to the important *asymmetry* we have already noticed between the two halves of the Kennedy/Nixon duology. Structurally, as we have seen, the title character of *JFK* appears on screen fleetingly in file footage, whereas the corresponding character in *Nixon* is incarnated in not only perhaps the best but also the most extensive dramatic performance in any of Stone's movies. Likewise, on the level of morality, Stone's Nixon cannot be seen—as one might have expected in advance—to be the pole of political evil in the same way that Kennedy is indeed the pole of political good.

Aristotle also says that the tragic hero must be "one who is highly renowned and prosperous—a personage like Oedipus, Thyestes, or other illustrious men of such families" (45–47). This generalization has held good throughout most of the history of the genre. It has been normally assumed that the loftiness of tragedy requires upper-class characters: as opposed to the "lower" and more democratic mode of comedy, in which persons of more humble station may appropriately appear. Shakespeare is, again, in this respect quite Aristotelian. His great tragic heroes—Brutus, Hamlet, Lear, Macbeth, Antony and Cleopatra, Coriolanus—not only occupy powerful positions and functions within their respective societies, but are all clearly high-*born* as well (the case of Othello is slightly ambiguous on this point). Since the age of the bourgeois-democratic revolutions, however, there have been various attempts to defy Aristotle's stricture and to create tragic protagonists of humbler birth and status.

The two most successful tragic figures in the entirety of American stage drama are good examples; and in both cases class is itself a major issue that is thematized within the plays in which they appear. Willy Loman, in Arthur Miller's *Death of a Salesman* (1949), is a middle- to lower-middle-class commercial traveler who fantasizes about rising far above his origins and attaining great wealth as his brother appears to have done. In the event, he is unable even to maintain his modest income and standard of consumption, and chooses death when it seems the only feasible alternative to destitution (or to reliance on the charity of his brother-in-law). Blanche DuBois in Tennessee Williams's *A Streetcar Named Desire* (1947)—perhaps the most frequently performed tragic heroine since Sophocles's Antigone and Shakespeare's Juliet and Cleopatra—is of shabby-genteel background and, like Willy, grows increasingly terrified by the downward financial path on which she is stuck. When she loses her job as a schoolteacher, she turns to reliance on her sexual wiles and fading good looks; the outcome is not physical death but a fate perhaps even worse, namely forced confinement to a Louisiana state mental institution.

Stone's Nixon is in certain respects a precise successor to Willy and Blanche; and Stone's film raises the whole issue of the class position of the tragic protagonist with considerable force and complexity. In a sense, an American president might seem to be socially equal—at least—to a Danish prince or a Scottish thane, and certainly superior to a traveling salesman or a schoolteacher. But the film takes a good deal of screen time to make clear that there is nothing noble in Nixon's origins; his background is commercial and petty-bourgeois. As we will see, one of the principal themes of *Nixon* is the nagging class insecurity of its title character. It is an insecurity that elevation to the highest political position in the world cannot cure or even much alleviate—and an insecurity that is always especially acute whenever Nixon is driven to compare his own situation to the family wealth and quasi-aristocratic social position enjoyed by John Kennedy.

A further characteristic to be considered of tragedy and the tragic hero is probably the most widely recognized of them all: a tragedy is a drama that ends with the death of its central figure. In Shakespeare this pattern is perfectly clear. In addition to the major Shakespearian tragic figures named above, even the protagonists of Shakespeare's more minor tragic plays—Titus Andronicus, Romeo and Juliet, Timon of Athens—all breathe their last before the final curtain falls. The same is generally true of the most important tragic protagonists created by Shakespeare's contemporaries, like the title characters of Christopher Marlowe's *Doctor Faustus* and of John Webster's *The Duchess of Malfi*. Yet there are, in fact, a number of exceptions to the generalization that a tragedy is defined by ending in death. Though the tragic hero is necessarily brought low in various ways, physical death is not invariably involved.

The most obvious example is *Oedipus the King*, often considered the pre-eminent masterwork of surviving ancient Athenian tragedy, and generally assumed by Aristotle, in the *Poetics*, to be paradigmatic of the genre. Sophocles's Oedipus is certainly miserable enough by the play's end. He is disgraced and has lost his royal position; his incestuous marriage is destroyed by his wife/mother Jocasta's suicide; he is blinded in both eyes by his own hand (self-castrated in the familiar Freudian symbolism); he is about to be exiled from his adoptive homeland; and he is in agonies of worry as to what life holds in store for his daughters, as they are now revealed to have sprung from such a terrible lineage. But he is, at any rate, still breathing. We have already noted a modern American example in Blanche DuBois. Her mind shattered by the traumas she has suffered (above all, being raped by her brother-in-law), she has, perhaps, a pretty limited life expectancy in the presumably miserable asylum to which she is bound; but she is on her feet as the curtain falls. Another important American example is Dick Diver in Scott Fitzgerald's tragic novel *Tender Is the Night* (1934). Unlike Fitzgerald's other great tragic protagonist—Jay Gatsby, who is shot to death and found as a floating corpse in his own swimming pool— Dick is very much alive as the narrative ends. But he is nonetheless an authentically tragic figure. Dick begins as a respected physician and psychiatrist who has stretching before him what looks to be a brilliant career. Marrying a rich and beautiful heiress who adores him, he becomes one half of a happy and extraordinarily glamorous, popular, and wealthy couple. By the end, he has become dispossessed of almost everything he ever had. His professional and social lives are both in shambles. He has lost his wife—and their children, and her money—and also the other woman with whom he betrayed her. To top things off, he is sunk in advanced alcoholism. One can almost imagine his envying the quick death of the great Gatsby.

Stone's Nixon is also alive at film's end (the end, that is, of the dramatic action proper, not counting a brief epilogue composed of some nonfictional archival footage of the real-life Nixon's departure from the White House and his funeral twenty years later). The conclusion of his story is his forced resignation of the presidency; and, in some ways, his situation might seem less dire than the situations of Oedipus or Blanche DuBois or Dick Diver. What, it could be asked, has he really lost? He will no longer be the president of the United States, but that, one might argue, simply puts him in the same boat with every other American except one. He is leaving the White House not for prison (which he considers at one point to be a serious possibility) or for foreign exile (Oedipus's fate) but for a comfortable existence in his private mansion in San Clemente, California. His long-faithful wife Pat (Joan Allen) remains loyally by his side. He has not lost, so far as one can tell, a single genuine friend (though it is, admittedly, unclear whether he ever *had* any to begin with). It is also worth pointing out that Nixon is leaving office with a large presidential pension guaranteed for life: something that, as the film makes clear, he would have lost if, instead of resigning, he had waited to be impeached by the House of Representatives and removed from office by the Senate, as he almost certainly would have been. When his situation is constructed in this way, one might be tempted to say that, if this is a tragic fate, then perhaps tragic fate need not be so very unpleasant after all.

But this construction of things, while accurate in a technical, factual way, is emotionally shallow and generically beside the point. The end of Nixon's presidency is also the end of his entire political career; and politics is the entirety of life for Nixon. Banishment from the electoral arena is thus a kind of symbolic and psychological death. Several scenes in the film make the Nixonian equation between politics and life quite expressly. In a relatively early scene, for example, Nixon and his top associates are discussing the loss to Kennedy on election night of 1960. The vote margin is very narrow, of course, particularly in Illinois and Texas, which together are essential for Kennedy's victory in the Electoral College; and there is some discussion as to whether the Nixon forces ought to demand recounts. Murray Chotiner (Fyvush Finkel), Nixon's most senior aide and his original mentor from the early days in California, counsels against this course. Attempting to cheer up the deeply depressed candidate, he says, "We'll get 'em next time, Dick. We'll get 'em next time!" As Nixon leaves the room, Herb Klein (Saul Rubinek), the campaign's press secretary, objects to Chotiner, "What makes you think there's gonna be a next time, Murray?" Chotiner picks up a Nixon campaign poster with a large photograph of the candidate, and replies decisively, "Because if he's not this Nixon, he's *nobody*." This is the real point. A Nixon banished from American politics is as much "nobody" as the corpse of Hamlet or Lear. Creon's self-description at the end of *Antigone*—"I who am not, I who am no more than no one"—would be perfectly applicable to Nixon out of office.[49] The comforts of what many people might consider Nixon's relatively enviable post-presidential life count for nothing with him. Nixon himself emphasizes the same idea in a scene set in 1963, when the 1964 campaign, in which Nixon is taking no part, is beginning to take shape. Talking with his New York law partner John Mitchell (E. G. Marshall)—who is eventually to become his campaign manager and later his attorney general—Nixon (though now earning more money than he has ever had before in his life) describes being out of politics as "hell." "I'll be mentally dead in two years," he says, "and physically dead in four."

This prediction does not actually come true. In two years, Nixon will in fact be campaigning for dozens of Republican candidates in the 1966 midterm elections—a phase of his career that the film elides—and in four years, of course, he captures the presidency. Even after resigning the White House and being banished from politics for good, Nixon does manage—as the film glancingly acknowledges in its epilogue—to survive physically for another two decades. But the film's psychological construction of its central character as the completely political being is sufficiently powerful so as to convince us that Nixon's ultimate fate in August 1974 is just as genuinely tragic as that of King Lear himself—who like Nixon, it might be pointed out, loses his position by failing to gauge accurately the socio-political forces around him (and who, as it happens, has provided Anthony Hopkins with another of his finest roles).[50] In order to analyze Stone's *Nixon* in detail—both as a work of cinematic art and as a portrait of the actual thirty-seventh president— it is essential to keep its tragic force, and its representation of its titular character as a tragic hero, steadily in view.

From *JFK* to *Nixon*

Despite the generic and other asymmetries between the conspiracy melodrama *JFK* and the psychological tragedy *Nixon*, the two films are, however, closely connected in several ways. Two levels of connection are most important. First, though the narrative of the later film is sharply different from that of the earlier one, *Nixon* makes clear its status as the second part of a duology by establishing a number of filiations with the plot of *JFK*. Though tragedy is the dominant form in the overdetermined generic structure of *Nixon*, the melodramatic conspiracy thriller of *JFK* is not entirely effaced: It maintains, instead, a haunting sort of afterlife in the later film's concern with the Kennedy assassination.

The assassination, which is present in one way or another throughout the entirety of the earlier film's plot, maintains a much more sporadic presence in the later one—and in ways that cohere with the conspiracy theory of *JFK*. One important example is the scene set on November 21, 1963, in which Nixon is a guest at the ranch of the Dallas multimillionaire (or perhaps billionaire) Jack Jones (Larry Hagman): the only important character in the film who is entirely fictional but who may be taken to personify the most reactionary elements of the US ruling class. Nixon is in Dallas in his private capacity as a corporate lawyer, but Jones has gathered together some of his business and political associates to try to convince the former vice-president to run in 1964 against JFK, whom they all hate bitterly; and they promise him unprecedented sums of campaign money if he will be their candidate. When Nixon demurs because "[n]obody's going to beat Kennedy in '64 with all the money in the world," one of Jones's friends, apparently a right-wing Cuban, suggests that perhaps Kennedy will not be running in 1964. "Not a chance," says Nixon. But the man (played by John Bedford Lloyd) has a sardonic smile on his face that—as Nixon seems to perceive—suggests he knows, or guesses, more than he is saying. Clearly *something* is being implied about the assassination that we know is coming the following day, but, as in *JFK*, questions are much more plentiful than answers. The rather crude and indiscreet men in Jones's living room seem an unlikely bunch of conspirators; but it is not implausible that some of them may have heard rumors about what is being planned. The following morning, as Nixon is flying back to New York (with some urgency, as though he suspects that something sinister is afoot in Dallas and wants to get out of town as quickly as possible), we see several shots of the presidential visit, including some nonfictional file footage of Kennedy's Dallas motorcade—a perfectly direct allusion to *JFK*.

An even more important scene shows a confrontation between Nixon, now president, and CIA Director Richard Helms (Sam Waterston). More than once, the film makes clear that Helms is (along with J. Edgar Hoover) one of the only two men in the Washington power establishment who is more than a match for the might of the presidency itself, and around whom Nixon therefore needs to tread carefully. Indeed, the film attributes this judgment to Nixon himself. Once, when Nixon is talking with H. R. Haldeman (James Woods)—his chief of staff and top aide—about how to contain the Watergate scandal, Haldeman suggests that, since most of the Watergate burglars have had CIA connections, the obvious course is just to blame the whole thing on the CIA and to let Helms take the fall. Nixon rejects the suggestion emphatically: "If there's anyone in this country who knows more than me, it's Hoover and Helms. And you don't fuck with Dick Helms—period."

In the scene that features Helms and Nixon together, Nixon has insisted on a *tête-à-tête* meeting in Helms's private office because he wants to use the CIA (illegally) for domestic spying on the antiwar movement and, even more, because he wants to retrieve any documents from his vice-presidential years that the CIA possesses and that explicitly connect him to what "X" in *JFK* calls Black Ops. Technically, of course, Nixon is Helms's superior—the chief executive who gives the orders and at whose pleasure the CIA Director serves—and at first Nixon tries to bluster as though Helms really were his subordinate. But both men know perfectly well that the formal hierarchy in which they are embedded does not accurately describe the actual power relations between them. Nixon's nervous awkwardness contrasts tellingly with Helms's utter *sang-froid* and seemingly effortless self-confidence. Once, pushing back against

Nixon's demands, Helms says, "President Kennedy threatened to smash the CIA into a thousand pieces. You could do the same." "I'm not Jack Kennedy," Nixon replies in a concessive tone. "Your agency is secure." Later in the conversation, as the two men are discussing Cuba policy, Nixon suggests that acceptance of Castro's regime in Cuba would be a small price to pay for permanently shattering the Sino-Soviet alliance. "So President Kennedy *thought*," sneers Helms in reply. Helms's first reference to Kennedy may have been slightly ambiguous—an apparent *non sequitur*, in context—but this one, coming on top of it, is pretty clearly a threat to have Nixon assassinated. Nixon himself instantly understands it as such. His face becomes a mask of fear, and he stammers with extreme agitation about what a terrible thing JFK's death was for the country—a notion that elicits no sympathy from Helms, who responds with a sarcastic "Yeah!".

Helms might best be described as a character whose "natural" homeland is rightfully *JFK*—where he never appears on screen, not even briefly in archival footage like so many other historical figures—but who has migrated from that film to the later one. Whereas Nixon as portrayed by Hopkins is, as we shall discuss further, a character of great moral complexity, Waterston's Helms is something close to pure evil in a way that fits well with the dichotomous moral structure of the first and far more melodramatic part of the duology. This point is nicely enforced in perhaps the most powerful visual touch in the scene between Nixon and Helms. In a close-up of Helms as he is gazing at some of the flowers that he grows in his office, his eyes very briefly become completely blank coal-black discs, as though we are looking into the damned, lost soul of Satan himself. In *JFK*, we never learn the identity of any of the top CIA and military conspirators who apparently planned the assassination. But, in *Nixon*—and allowing for the deliberately cryptic style in which the very powerful speak to one another about forbidden matters—Helms all but openly proclaims himself to have been one of them. We are bound to remember, of course, that one of the on-screen legends at the end of *JFK* informs us that Richard Helms was, in 1963, the CIA's Director of Covert Operations.

So *Nixon* acknowledges and endorses the conspiracy melodrama of *JFK* even while itself adopting a generic structure quite different from that of the earlier film. The second way in which the later film binds itself to the earlier one concerns the importance that John Kennedy himself assumes within the detailed psychological portrait of Richard Nixon.

As a serious and well-read student of history, Nixon naturally has occasion to reflect on a number of his presidential precursors—for instance Theodore Roosevelt, whom Nixon particularly admires for his insistence on being strenuously "in the arena"; Franklin Roosevelt, generally considered the creator of the modern American presidency; and Lyndon Johnson, Nixon's immediate predecessor. But three other former presidents seem uppermost in the thinking of Stone's Nixon, their importance visually emblematized by the prominence and frequency with which we see their official portraits on the walls of the Nixon White House. One is Lincoln, the first Republican president and Nixon's all-time hero and role model. As the film once explicitly points out, Lincoln and Nixon both began as obscure small-town attorneys; and, as the Watergate crisis deepens, Nixon's younger daughter Julie (Annabeth Gish) tells her father that he, like Lincoln, has brought his country back from civil war. Another president that especially occupies Nixon's mind is Eisenhower, Nixon's most important patron. Ike's decision to make and (after a scandal over Senator Nixon's slush fund) to keep Nixon as his running mate in 1952 was essential to the political rise that has allowed Nixon to capture the summit of American politics. The third, and psychologically by far the most important president for Nixon, is JFK.

In the metaphorical terms of Nixon's political family romance, we might say that Lincoln is the ancestral forefather and Eisenhower the father. Kennedy, then, is the sibling (the *younger* sibling, indeed), and the 1960 presidential contest can be understood as a kind of symbolic sibling rivalry. It is no accident that Nixon, recalling the early friendship of the two men when they were freshmen members of the US House, should, as we have noted, describe them as having been "like brothers." (It is also no accident that the film, in its scenes set during Nixon's childhood, is careful to make clear that no serious rivalry was ever possible between Richard and his *actual* brothers, so clearly superior was he in intelligence and discipline. But Tony Goldwyn, the actor who plays Richard's older brother Harold, is made up to bear some physical resemblance to John Kennedy, and his character—handsome, self-confident, outgoing, secular, and strongly attracted to the opposite sex—has a Kennedyesque connotation.) As the 1960 election returns come in, it becomes clear that, at least as far as Nixon is concerned, the fraternal bond between JFK and Nixon is now less like that between Moses and Aaron, or between Agamemnon and Menelaus, than like that between Cain and Abel.

In the scene set on election night of 1960, Nixon seems less interested in the discussion among his aides as to whether to ask for recounts in Illinois and Texas than in his own obsessive personal competition with Kennedy. "Goes to Harvard," he complains. "His father hands him everything on a silver platter. . . . And then he steals from me. Heh, and he says I have no class. And they love him for it." For such a completely political creature as Nixon, narrowly losing the supreme political prize would, of course, have been painful enough in any case. More than 68 million votes were cast in the 1960 election, and, if just 27,000 of them in two states had gone (or been counted) differently, the White House would have been his. But what appears even more galling for Nixon is that he has been defeated by his old friend and coeval, and not fairly. Part of the perceived injustice is the supposed vote-stealing in Texas and Illinois (as Nixon in the film insists, and as Nixon's admirers in real life have been consistently maintaining for six decades). Yet even worse for Nixon are the advantages that Kennedy has enjoyed from birth. The personal struggle between the two men is, on Nixon's side, a kind of petty-bourgeois class struggle as well. Immediately following the scene on election night, the film offers black-and-white flashbacks of Nixon's earlier life in Whittier, California. We see the unimpressive wooden grocery store in which the Nixon family earned its modest living when Richard was a boy; and we also see him as a young man, ineptly trying to play football on the Whittier College team. The contrast between Nixon's lower-middle-class origins and the Kennedy centimillions is too obvious to need stating, as, indeed, is the contrast between Whittier College and Harvard. In perhaps the most bitter words of Nixon's election-night rant about Kennedy as "a guy who's got everything," he complains that, "All my life they've been sticking it to me. Not the right clothes, not the right schools, not the right family." Grammatically, the personal pronoun *they* (in "they've") has no clear antecedent. Nixon is pluralizing JFK so that he stands, in Nixon's mind, not only for himself and for his own wealthy, glamorous, and well-educated family, but also for what Nixon throughout the film will denounce as "the elite" generally. In a way, this denunciation seems absurd, because, rationally considered, no one in US society could possibly be more "elite" than the leader of the Republican Party. But Kennedy, for Nixon, has come to personify all the advantages that his own modest origins have denied him. After JFK's death, Nixon's Kennedy obsession is easily transferred to JFK's younger brothers Robert and (then) Edward, the only political rivals that ever seriously worry Stone's Nixon from 1963 onwards. (Hubert Humphrey and George McGovern, Nixon's actual Democratic opponents in the 1968 and 1972 presidential contests, respectively, are barely ever seen or mentioned.)

Nixon's obsession with JFK in *Nixon* offers, then, an alternative view of the thirty-fifth president from that presented in the earlier half of the duology: Garrison's admiring, indeed hero-worshipping, view of JFK as the father-leader who, had he lived, would have saved America from the Vietnam War and from other atrocities perpetrated by the national-security state is contrasted with Nixon's resentful and somewhat paranoid view of him as the overprivileged embodiment of a system responsible for Nixon's own personal failures (of which the electoral loss in 1960 is the most dramatic pre-Watergate instance). In yet another aspect of the asymmetry between the two films, Garrison—who, of course, historically had no personal relationship with JFK—takes a mainly political view of his hero, while Nixon's view of Kennedy is not particularly political or ideological at all. Like the elderly real-life Nixon who conversed with Monica Crowley, Stone's Nixon does not, for the most part, see Kennedy as clearly opposed to himself on the level of policies and ideas. His struggle with Kennedy is much more personal than that. The two men were once, as Nixon says, "like brothers," and it is the fraternal relation gone bad that produces the most bitter enmity (just as civil war is the cruelest kind of war, as President Nixon comments to Chairman Mao Zedong [Ric Young] in a later scene). This is a Biblical insight, one suggested when the Book of Genesis records humanity's first murder as taking place between brothers.

But—to dwell for a moment on the Cain-and-Abel analogy—who has murdered whom? Kennedy's "unfair" defeat of Nixon in the 1960 race is a kind of metaphorical homicide from Nixon's viewpoint, but, after 1963, it is Kennedy himself who actually lies dead and buried, while Nixon goes on to capture the presidential prize of which Kennedy had deprived him. Is Nixon in any sense responsible for JFK's death? There are several ways that the question might be considered. According to the ethical logic of the New Testament ("But I say unto you, That whosoever looketh on a woman to lust after her hath committed adultery with her already in his heart"—Matthew 5:28), hatred like Nixon's for Kennedy could be regarded as psychological or symbolic murder, as the moral equivalent of actual killing. Then again, on the plane of empirical fact, we recall that—though Stone, in both films, is careful never to associate Nixon directly with the conspiracy to kill Kennedy—Garrison, in his summation to the jury in *JFK*, does imply that President Nixon (because of his administration's refusal to cooperate with Garrison's investigation) might be considered an accomplice after the fact in the crime for which Clay Shaw is being prosecuted. Finally, and most telling of all, President Nixon himself, referring to the secret government and the Black Ops with which he has been involved since he was vice-president, at one point says, "Whoever killed Kennedy came from this thing *we* created, this beast" (emphasis added—the sentence is heard on a portion of a White House tape that history knows as occupied only by the famously mysterious eighteen-and-a-half-minute blank gap).

Nixon: Personal Tragedy

The deeply personal nature of Nixon's rivalry with Kennedy in *Nixon* is one way that the film, in yet a further instance of asymmetry, is far more personal overall than the earlier installment of the duology. In *JFK*, we see nothing of Kennedy's private life and not a great deal of Garrison's. In the later film, we see a fair amount of Nixon away from the office and the business of public life: mainly in the flashback scenes of the younger Nixon in Whittier and in scenes from the Nixon marriage on the several occasions that we see Dick and Pat *tête-à-tête*. Such scenes help to make the film a more personal and individual-centered narrative than its far more directly and exclusively political predecessor. Since there is relatively little of a historical record on which these scenes could be based (though there is some), they are also the parts of the film in which Stone (and his co-screenwriters Christopher Wilkinson and Stephen Rivele) may be assumed to have exercised maximum creative freedom.

For example, the scene that introduces us to the Nixon family's grocery store also shows us the film's youngest version of its titular character. The twelve-year-old Nixon (Corey Carrier) appears bright, alert, conscientious, hard-working, and considerably more handsome than Anthony Hopkins made up as the adult Nixon, or, for that matter, than the adult Nixon in real life. As we meet young Dick, his older brother Harold is in the midst of a difficult dispute with their father Frank Nixon (Tom Bower) over Harold's request for a suit in which to take a favorite girlfriend to a dance (for a suit is not an inconsiderable luxury in the Nixon family economy). The young Richard does what he can to smooth over the domestic tensions, just as one day he will be negotiating for the United States with China and the Soviet Union. In a slightly later scene, we see him as a college student (David Barry Gray, appearing even more handsome than Corey Carrier) on the Whittier College gridiron, where his lack of athletic talent is counterpointed by his stubborn determination to play football at all costs. Gray's face stoically registers serious pain as Nixon is repeatedly pummeled by other players. "Worst athlete I've ever seen," comments the coach (Jack Wallace) to an associate. "But he's got guts."

Stone thus portrays the younger Nixon—the pre-Hopkins Nixon, as we might put it—as a fairly appealing character in several ways. The all-American good looks of Carrier and Gray connote the virtues conventionally associated with the stereotype of the all-American boy: who is normally imagined as having sprung from economically modest circumstances but possessing the qualities needed to rise above his origins in the land of opportunity. We see the young Dick Nixon uncomplainingly performing routine work in his family's store, even while displaying the intellectual quickness and the insight into the interpersonal relations around him that suggest he is not destined to spend his whole life stocking grocery shelves. These are, indeed, precisely the characteristics that might well be expected in a successful politician. The same is true of the qualities of Stone's Nixon in the Whittier College football program. That the brief shots we see of Nixon being painfully knocked around on the gridiron are entirely typical of his sporting career is made plain when another player (Ian Calip), in a voice that conveys more pity than contempt, describes Nixon's entire participation in the football program as "four years of being a tackling dummy"—a phrase that the adult Nixon himself, as president, will adapt in a rare attempt at self-depreciating humor. One may attribute his tenacity to courage ("guts"), as the coach does, or, alternatively (as we will see), to masochism. But, in any case, the ability to take punishment and come back for more is an indispensable political virtue. Even, or rather especially, the most successful politicians—and Nixon, from his first race in 1946 until his first defeat in 1960, was about as successful as it is possible for an electoral politician to be—are likely to be on the receiving end of more personal aggression than can be found on any football field.

There is one scene of the young—in this case, the twelve-year-old—Nixon in which, however, he appears anything but all-American. His mother Hannah Nixon (Mary Steenburgen) sits him down for a stern talk. She accuses him of being unduly influenced by his brother Harold's un-Biblical worldliness and, more specifically, of accepting from Harold a corn-silk cigarette. The detail that the cigarette is made of corn silk is a nicely casual allusion to the Nixon family's economic circumstances; for, in America during the early twentieth century, corn silk was a common tobacco substitute for those unable to afford the real thing. But the deeper significance of the cigarette is that Hannah considers mere possession of it to be a sin of almost unspeakable heinousness: and, as we will discuss very shortly, she enforces this moral judgment with deadly seriousness.

During the real-life Nixon's final morning in the White House, in one of the most vividly remembered parts of his farewell address to his staff (and a part prominently featured in the Stone film), Nixon said that his mother, by then deceased, had been "a saint." Doubtless many viewers of the televised speech considered this to be a meaningless political platitude. After all, what politician, even at the end of his career, would *not* describe his own mother as a saint? In fact, however, the biographical evidence makes clear that, long before the world had heard of her favorite son, Hannah Nixon *did* have quite a reputation for saintliness. She was, for instance, known for extraordinary charity in the sense of alms. More than a few of America's homeless and hungry passed through Whittier when Richard Nixon was growing up (especially after the Wall Street crash of 1929), and many of them knew that the Quaker saint Hannah was usually good for a meal and a hand-out: as, indeed, the Stone film indicates in one of the Whittier scenes.[51]

The real point of the scene of the corn-silk cigarette is that there are aspects of saintliness considerably less attractive than material generosity. Hannah's furious moralism is expressed not in the physical violence that (as another Whittier scene indicates, and as the adult President Nixon will approvingly recall many years later) her husband favors, but in a considerably more frightening exercise of *psychic* violence. Sitting calmly in a chair and never raising her voice, Hannah, with simple words and subtle facial expressions, threatens to withhold the maternal affection that is clearly all-important to young Richard; and she soon reduces him to a quivering jelly of a boy. "Remember, I see into thy soul," she assures him, as though she possesses virtually God-like powers of clairvoyance. "Thee may fool the world, even thy father. But not me, Richard— never me." Literally kneeling before her and with an expression of abject fear on his face—perhaps even greater fear, indeed, than he will display years later when Richard Helms, with a subtlety that does not quite match Hannah's, threatens to have him killed—he replies, "Mother, think of me always as thy faithful dog." His choice of words precisely expresses the dehumanization that his mother's saintly bullying has forced upon him. Saintliness, as Nietzsche knew, can be a terrifying thing.

The Whittier scenes of *Nixon* (filmed mainly in black and white in accordance with the venerable cinematic convention that the world actually looked that way before the predominance of color film) thus suggest that the personal tragedy of Richard Nixon was prefigured long before his political career began. Nixon as a boy and as a young man clearly possesses well above-average abilities and some admirable moral qualities. One can easily imagine him growing up to be the Nixon who will negotiate successfully with Chairman Mao and, for that matter—though the Stone film ignores this part of his career—the Nixon who in 1957 will work for civil rights with Martin Luther King. But the young Nixon is not only subjected to appalling domestic violence but comes to internalize and glory in it: whether it be the physical beatings that, in the White House, he will fondly remember as taking place in his "Ohio father's wood shed," or, much worse, the moralistic violence of the saintly mother to which he responds with such abjection. Years before he enters Whittier College, his masochism has well qualified him to be a tackling dummy. Masochism, in Nixon's case, is the *hamartia* that Aristotle identifies in the tragic hero: the fatal flaw or (as some scholars prefer to translate the Greek term) the mistake that leads to disaster.

We need to remember, though, that, as psychoanalysis has always insisted, masochism is necessarily *sado*masochism. Sadism and masochism are not dichotomous opposites but inter-related and complementary aspects of the same personality type.[52] In *Nixon*, we do not actually see the sadistic side of Nixon when he is young. But, many years later, in 1972, Chairman Mao will shrewdly diagnose the "hunger" in Nixon's soul that has led him to slaughter "millions of Vietnamese."

But remaining, for the time being, on the more personal level of this tragic dramatic narrative, we may turn to the film's scenes from the Nixon marriage. In real life, Pat Nixon was (along with Mamie Eisenhower and perhaps Melania Trump) the least publicly visible of America's modern first ladies. She possessed neither the glamor of a Jackie Kennedy (maybe the most beautiful first lady in American history) nor the strong outgoing personality of a Betty Ford, a Nancy Reagan, or a Michelle Obama. There was no worthy, uncontroversial cause with which she was prominently identified as Laura Bush was with literacy, or Rosalyn Carter with mental health, or Lady Bird Johnson with highway beautification. Personally detesting the world of politics—she thought she was marrying a small-town attorney when the Nixons wed in 1940—Pat Nixon loyally appeared in public with her husband whenever political duty required but otherwise kept a very low profile. She was there for her husband's farewell speech in 1974, in which he elaborately praised his dead parents but said not a single word about the woman who was standing beside him, and who had been publicly standing beside him since 1946. From her teenage years, though, Pat Nixon (or Thelma Catherine Ryan, as she was born) had always had a strong desire to travel the world, and that must have been at least one reward that her marriage brought her.

Out of this publicly faint figure, Stone's *Nixon* constructs a woman who is intelligent, attractive, and self-confident, if also rather frustrated about life in general. In a film that, like *JFK*, boasts a large gallery of extraordinary performances, Joan Allen delivers perhaps the most powerful next to Hopkins's own (both were nominated for Oscars). In striking contrast to the image of the quietly passive political wife that the real-life Pat Nixon presented to the world, the Pat Nixon of the movie challenges her husband as nobody else who is personally close to him ever dares to do; and she does so from a position of apparent psychic "normality" that aligns her far more with the implied viewer than with the tragic protagonist, with his obsessions and oddities, to whom she is married. At some points, indeed, Pat Nixon—in an implicit tribute that the film pays to the history of tragedy as a genre—functions rather like a one-woman Greek chorus.

In one key scene, President Nixon is preparing to travel from the White House to his vacation home in Key Biscayne, Florida— by himself, though his wife wishes to accompany him. When she asks why they cannot go together, his brutally revealing answer is, "Because I have to relax." She reminds him of the early days of their courtship, when he was so eager always to be with her that he even drove her on dates with other boys (a detail taken directly from the biographical record). "It was a long time ago," he replies, with little emotion in his voice. Sitting on a bed beside her husband, Pat then tries some tentatively seductive moves, and begins kissing her husband on the hand. The president withdraws, saying "I don't need that," and then adds—even more tellingly, and using precisely the same words that he has earlier used to Richard Helms—"I'm not Jack Kennedy."

At this point, then, the scene has clearly established a sadistic element in Richard Nixon's marital relation. The sadistic side of his sadomasochism is evident. No physical violence is involved, nor is there—here or anywhere else in the film—any hint of such a thing on Nixon's part: even though, interestingly, there is serious biographical scholarship that suggests the thirty-seventh president, in real life, to have indeed been a wife-beater.[53] But Stone's Richard Nixon is always more his mother's than his father's son. It is the techniques of emotional withholding that we have seen Hannah Nixon employ—here compounded with overtly sexual rejection— that are decisive in Nixon's sadistic drive to establish superiority over his wife. The masochism that years earlier had allowed him to humiliate himself by serving as Pat's chauffeur while she was dating his own rivals (visually illustrated in flashback) is now comple- mented by sadism of a specifically sexual, or rather anti-sexual, kind. Stone's Pat Nixon is consistently a fairly sympathetic character, and there is no suggestion, at this point, of her being anything other than a loving wife. Joan Allen, in the scene under discussion, consistently looks at Anthony Hopkins with tender and sincere, though frustrated, love, and the script gives her several lines that make the point explicitly: for instance, relatively late in the scene, "It took me a long time to fall in love with you, Dick. But I did." But the president rebuffs her every expression, whether verbal or bodily, of wifely affection.

The rather surprising remark with which he accompanies physical rejection of his wife's romantic advances—"I'm not Jack Kennedy"—is particularly significant. On one level, of course, this is yet another expression of Nixon's general obsession with JFK. On another, it is an allusion to John Kennedy's robust sexual appetite and compulsive womanizing: things that were mostly kept from common view during the Kennedy Administration (journalists, in those days, did not write about the sex lives of living politicians) and, indeed, things never acknowledged in Stone's *JFK*, but things always well-known to Washington insiders like the Nixons (and by 1995 well-known to the public at large). On a deeper level, however, Nixon really means much the same thing here that he means when he utters exactly the same sentence to Richard Helms: that he is not just a different kind of man from Jack Kennedy but a different kind of *president*. The completely political being, for whom exile from the political arena would be (and will be) a kind of living death, Nixon, as he refuses to reciprocate his wife's love, immediately explains and contextualizes this rejection in explicitly political terms. When Pat, Greek-chorus-like, poses a question that might occur to the typical viewer—"You have everything you ever wanted—you earned it—why can't you just enjoy it?"—her husband explains that enjoyment of any usual sort is precluded by the political circumstances of the time. The country, says Nixon, is "in deep, deep, deep trouble," and he makes clear that he is uniquely qualified and positioned to save the situation. Thundering against "the elite" in various of its forms, he seems to suggest that the political battle leaves no time—and perhaps no energy—for lovemaking. This is the dialectic of sadomasochism. Nixon is sadistic toward the wife whose love he refuses to return and toward the political enemies whom he yearns to defeat, and at the same time masochistic toward the moral imperatives of the general situation that preclude enjoyment and compel him to sleepless struggle. Yet (what Nixon will finally come to see in the moment of catastrophe) it is just this struggle against political enemies that, with perfect tragic irony, will ultimately function as the engine of masochistic self-destruction.

If, however, the personal situation of the Nixon marriage is, for the president, understandable only in terms of politics and political duty, the political is, in a reciprocal reduction, centered completely on his own person. The sadomasochistic concentration on self at times seems virtually absolute. As one of the scene's most revealing exchanges has it:

RICHARD NIXON:	They're playing for keeps, Buddy. You know—the press, the kids, the liberals out there. They're out there trying to figure out how to tear me down.
PAT NIXON:	They're all your enemies?
RICHARD NIXON:	Yes!
PAT NIXON:	You personally?
RICHARD NIXON:	Yes! Listen: this is about me. Why can't you understand that—I mean, you of all people? It's not the war—it's Nixon! It's not Vietnam—it's Nixon! They want to destroy Nixon! If I expose myself just the slightest bit, they'll tear my insides out. You want that? You know? You want to see that, Buddy? It's not pretty.

| PAT NIXON: | Sometimes I think that's what you want, Dick. |
| RICHARD NIXON [WITH FURY IN HIS VOICE]: | What the hell are you saying? Are you drunk? Jesus, you sound just like them now. |

The sadomasochism in Nixon's image of political *agon* as physical disembowelment is evident enough, and Pat, in her final comment quoted above, acutely grasps her husband's masochistic side. It is no surprise—it seems, indeed, almost inevitable—that, before the scene is done, the ultimate representative, for Nixon, of ethical authority, of the punitive superego before whom he must self-laceratingly abase himself, should make her (posthumous) presence felt. Explaining the absolute requirement that he serve as America's moral savior, Nixon says, "Mother would have expected no less of me."

Nixon's rejection of his wife, his withholding of affection, takes its toll on the Nixon marriage as the film presents it; and the growing estrangement between the couple unfolds on a track parallel to that of the president's political self-destruction in the Watergate scandal. In yet another instance of the huge influence that *Citizen Kane* has had on Oliver Stone, an important later scene of Dick and Pat together at dinner is directly modeled, both visually and in emotional tone, on a similar scene in Welles's movie. The Nixons sit at opposite ends of a long dining table, like Charles Foster Kane and his first wife, and, like them, converse in mutual irritation and incomprehension. Pat wants to know how her husband intends to navigate some of the political and legal challenges posed by Watergate; but he makes clear that he does not intend to discuss this or any other serious matter with her. "Why are you cutting yourself off from the rest of us?" she asks. "Can't we discuss this?"—again, questions that might well occur to the viewer. But, when she warns him that he is on a path that will lead to his own destruction, he responds by impatiently ringing a bell for a White House servant, whom he instructs to remove Mrs. Nixon's dishes from the table. Rubbing salt in the psychic wounds he is inflicting, he notes that the Soviet leader Leonid Brezhnev is coming soon for a summit meeting, and (referring also to those members of the Ervin Committee in the US Senate who are aggressively investigating Watergate) Nixon says, "I don't want to deal with *them* and *him* and *you*"—expressly placing his own wife in the same category as a superpower adversary and his domestic political opponents. Utterly exasperated, Pat assures her husband, "I won't interfere with you anymore. I'm finished trying." But she is further amazed and horrified when the president responds with the shockingly cruel two-word answer, "Thank you." The scene ends as Pat Nixon fulfills with complete precision her role as the Greek chorus of the tragedy: "Dick, sometimes I understand why they hate you."

Not long thereafter, the former White House counsel John Dean (David Hyde Pierce) testifies to the Ervin Committee about Nixon's illegal cover-up of the Watergate burglaries. Alexander Butterfield—a former top aide to Haldeman, and, according to some real-life rumors, Richard Helms's secret spy in the White House—testifies to the committee about the hitherto secret tapes of Nixon's conversations. These are the tapes that will eventually reveal, among other things, the "smoking gun" that establishes the president's criminality in the cover-up beyond all reasonable doubt and leads directly to his forced resignation. (The crucial conversation is one that took place on June 23, 1972, in which Nixon orders Haldeman to try to persuade the CIA to impede the FBI's investigation into the Watergate burglaries.) As Dick sits in a small White House room, listening to some of the tapes, Pat wanders in—drinking (she holds in her hand what appears to be a glass of whisky), somewhat drunk (as she soon admits), yet nonetheless quite lucid in her speech. The marital relation is now at its furthest point of estrangement, and Pat not only confronts her husband with open hostility but at some points appears to align herself overtly with his political enemies: "I remember Alger Hiss. I know how ugly you can be. You're capable of anything." (It needs to be recalled that, though Hiss was criminally convicted, political and scholarly opinion has always remained sharply divided as to whether Nixon's career-making investigation of him was in fact the persecution of an innocent man.) Pat suggests to her husband that he should burn the tapes; and, when he explains that one cannot legally destroy evidence, she laughingly sneers at the idea that obedience to the law would play any part in his decision-making. When the president, with perfect Sophoclean irony, expresses confidence that no one, including Pat, will ever learn what is on the tapes, she delivers perhaps her most powerful verbal blow of all: "And what would I find out that I haven't known for *years*?" She takes her glass of booze and leaves, again advising her husband to burn the tapes.

The dead Hannah Nixon has appeared earlier in the scene, in what is probably meant to be her son's remembering. But, after Pat's departure, Hannah appears again, in what now seems to be full-fledged hallucination, asking, "What has changed in you, Richard?" His response is to fall violently ill with a near-fatal attack of phlebitis and viral pneumonia. The *hamartia* of sadomasochism that the film traces to the mother-complex of Nixon's childhood has now led, at least metaphorically, to a medical condition that brings him close to physical death. It has also led, far more directly, to what appears to be the destruction of any authentic marital relationship with his wife (though she remains with him and appears genuinely distraught when he is near death in the hospital). Most consequentially of all, it will lead to the living death that is the destruction of Nixon's public career and his expulsion from the political arena. Pat Nixon notes the irony that her extremely secretive husband, who could not trust even those closest to him, nonetheless made, with the tapes, a record "for the whole world" of his private dealings—and, unlike him, she foresees that these creations of his are bound to destroy him politically. On this point the film's Pat and the film itself are in good accord with the historical record. Though counterfactual speculations can never be proved or disproved, it seems extremely unlikely that Watergate would have ended anything like as disastrously for Nixon as it actually did, had the White House tapes not provided irrefutable answers to the question that Senator Howard Baker of the Ervin Committee asked again and again during the committee's hearings in the summer of 1973: "What did the president know, and when did he know it?" Nixon, historically and in the movie, provides the instrument of his own demise.[54]

Nixon: National Tragedy

The personal tragedy of anyone so completely defined by his political identity as Stone's Richard Nixon necessarily, as we have seen, encompasses many transpersonal political situations. But it is now time to examine the larger political scene of *Nixon* more closely, and to analyze how Stone's Nixon makes for tragedy not only for himself but for America—in several ways, indeed, which are not only different from one another but in certain respects even opposed. For Stone's Nixon, as both a villain and a hero, is as morally ambiguous as any Aristotelian protagonist ought to be.

The idea of Nixon as a tragic figure on the political stage of his country and of the world is, in fact, explicitly presented in the film itself: and by the only two characters who might be considered as (in different ways) his political peers. One is Leonid Brezhnev (Boris Sichkin). Though the Soviet leader is a geopolitical adversary, Nixon seems to regard him also as a colleague and perhaps even, in a strange way, as a friend. Brezhnev, after all, is, besides Nixon himself, the only other person on the planet who knows what it is to lead a superpower. They are the only two members of the most exclusive club in the world. During a summer 1973 summit meeting at the White House, the two men address one another in a cordial, first-name way. At one point, Nixon excuses himself from their conversation to consult about the worrying news of Dean's testimony before the Ervin Committee, leaving Brezhnev to chat with Soviet Foreign Minister Andrei Gromyko (Fima Noveck). The two Soviets are thoroughly familiar with the domestic political situation in the United States, and Brezhnev comments of Nixon (as the subtitles translate the Russian), "Tragic, isn't it? He had the world in the palm of his hand." Later, Brezhnev's words are echoed with almost eerie precision by Henry Kissinger (Paul Sorvino). Kissinger, once described by Nixon as "my equal in many ways," has been his only real partner in the foreign-policy initiatives of the Nixon Administration that are the president's supreme pride and joy, and the only person whose understanding of geopolitics he respects as being comparable to his own. (Nixon's attitude toward his own State Department is one of open contempt.) As the Nixon presidency collapses, Kissinger, employing rather Aristotelian language, remarks to a White House associate, "It's a tragedy, because he had greatness in his grasp. But he had the defects of his qualities." Kissinger later tells Nixon himself that his downfall is "a fate of Biblical proportions."

Brezhnev and Kissinger are naturally uninterested in Nixon's marriage or the state of his health. Their concern is with geopolitics. And the movie's two scenes that directly represent geopolitical diplomacy are those that show President Nixon at his best. In the scene with Brezhnev at the White House, Nixon is understandably distracted by reports of Dean's testimony (a distraction visually suggested as scenes of the testimony are sometimes intercut with and sometimes superimposed on the footage of the superpower leaders). Nonetheless, the president manages to handle himself and his Soviet adversary pretty well. Brezhnev is clearly worried about the anti-Soviet implications of the emerging Sino-American entente that Nixon appears to be constructing with Mao Zedong, and he tells Nixon of a conversation he claims to have had with Mao about a decade earlier. Mao had expressed a desire to acquire nuclear weapons (which of course he now possesses), and supposedly said that he had little to fear from nuclear war: for, as Brezhnev reports Mao saying, even if 400 million Chinese perished in a nuclear exchange, there would still be 300 million left. Brezhnev's point is that anyone who could thus casually contemplate such mass death is a monster and a lunatic, and he asks how Nixon can possibly want such a man for an ally. Nixon parries the point skillfully, indeed unanswerably: "Well, he was your ally for twenty years, Leonid." Brezhnev chuckles in an appreciative, concessive way. "Yes, yes, Dick," he says in English—and goes on to maintain that nothing must prevent the success of the SALT II treaty to limit the American and Soviet nuclear arsenals. Nixon, who desires SALT II as much as Brezhnev does, does not disagree with his Soviet counterpart's contention that peace between the superpowers is attainable.

The earlier (February 1972) scene in Beijing with Nixon, Kissinger, and Mao himself is a bit longer and rather more complex. Unlike the relatively straightforward Brezhnev, Mao seems deliberately hard to pin down, by turns acting rude, cynical, penetrating, and impish. When Kissinger attempts to flatter the chairman by telling him that his writings have changed the world, Mao brusquely turns the compliment aside with the epithet "Bullshit!" (as Mao's translator renders the Mandarin Chinese) and insists that his writings mean absolutely nothing. He then says that what really interests him is learning Kissinger's own "secret," which turns out to be "how a fat man gets so many girls." Kissinger helpfully replies, "Power, Mr. Chairman, is the ultimate aphrodisiac"—an insight with which he must surely assume Mao (whose translator is an attractive young woman) to be already thoroughly familiar. In a different exchange, Mao tells Nixon that he "voted" for him in 1968.

Nixon jovially replies that he assumes the Chinese leader chose him as the lesser of two evils, and at that pleasantry Mao suddenly turns deadly serious: "You are too modest, Mr. Nixon. You are as evil as I am. We are the new emperors. We are both from poor families, and others pay to feed the hunger in us.[55] In my case, millions of reactionaries. In your case, millions of Vietnamese." Mao's mercurial style of talk—his frequent refusal to say the predictable thing, and his sudden switching from one sort of discourse to another—is perhaps to be understood as a way of probing his American interlocutors' adroitness, their ability to respond. If it is such a test, Nixon passes with flying colors. Without ever violating diplomatic politesse, Nixon manages to focus the conversation on the project with which he is really concerned, the opening of US foreign policy to the People's Republic of China as a way of outflanking the USSR. When he shares with Mao the American maxim that the enemy of one's enemy is one's friend, the Chinese leader heartily agrees; and Mao makes his own sympathies clear by denouncing both the Russians and the Vietnamese as "dogs." Later, as Air Force One is flying Nixon and his associates home, Dick sums up the achievement of the trip to Pat with what the film seems to regard as at least somewhat justified pride: "Just think of the life that Mao has led. In '52 I called him a monster [in a speech that the movie has earlier shown in flashback]. Now he could be our most important ally. Only Nixon could have done that."

Despite the widespread view of Nixon as the Mordred of modern US presidents, it has long been conventional among journalists and historians to allow him some significant positive credit for his grasp of geopolitics and, in particular, for his opening to China and his détente with the Soviet Union. Though *Nixon* does not unequivocally endorse this view, it does seem to permit it to a certain degree. Certainly the skillful, self-assured Nixon in dialogue with Mao and with Brezhnev compares favorably with the film's general portrayal of the adult Nixon as awkward, insecure, paranoid, and above all sadomasochistic. The closest thing that the film offers to an explicitly political judgment on the matter comes toward the very end, in some voice-over narration in the epilogue spoken (uncredited) by Oliver Stone himself: "In his [Nixon's] absence, Russia and the United States returned to a decade of high-budget military expansion and near-war." Historically, there were, indeed, many Americans who, through the 1980s and 1990s, looked back to Nixon's foreign policy with more nostalgia than they may once have thought possible (one of them was George McGovern, who was the target of many of the Watergate crimes and whose antiwar presidential candidacy Nixon crushed in the 1972 election). Perhaps, the film seems to suggest, the smart, earnest, well-intentioned boy portrayed by Corey Carrier—a still photograph of whose fresh, appealing face as the child Nixon appears just after the film's epilogue and before the final credits—really did grow up to do some good in the world. Perhaps the "peace at the center" that Nixon, in his farewell speech to his staff—a speech memorably spoken by Anthony Hopkins just prior to the epilogue—upholds as the ultimate Quaker value really did influence his policies concerning the peace of the world.

Yet this positive view, which the film at least teases us to consider, can be decisively undercut by a single word that *Nixon* seldom allows us to forget and that is, indeed, arguably the central single word in the entire Oliver Stone cinematic *oeuvre*: Vietnam. We are never allowed to overlook the millions of slaughtered Vietnamese referred to by Mao.[56] The conversation between Nixon and Mao ends with Mao cryptically suggesting, "The real war is in us. History is a symptom of our disease." But what has not been at all cryptic in the chairman's remarks is the enmity he has expressed toward the Vietnamese and the Soviets—with the clear implication that ferocious American prosecution of the Vietnam War will not only prove no obstacle to forming the nascent Sino-American alliance but may even itself be one of the benefits that Mao hopes to gain from the entente. If the enemy of one's enemy is one's friend, Mao will be glad to see his enemies weakened by his new friend (the Soviets weakened in the sense that the USSR is the main geopolitical supporter of North Vietnam and the South Vietnamese National Liberation Front). The point is visually illustrated as the scene of the president and the chairman conversing dissolves into apparently archival footage of US planes dropping bombs on Hanoi and the Vietnamese countryside. This is the so-called "Christmas bombing" of December 1972, taking place about ten months after the Nixon-Mao meeting in Beijing. Spectacular shots of death and destruction are pretty clearly meant to be seen as the direct outcome of the meeting between the two world leaders immediately preceding. Lest the viewer may be slow to recall how horrendous the bombing actually was, voice-over narration (evidently meant to represent impersonal and "objective" journalistic comment) explicitly reminds us that President Nixon "delivered more tonnage than was used in Dresden in World War II." The anonymous voice adds, "It is without doubt the most brutal bombing in American history."

This scene is far from the only one to illustrate that what we maintained in the previous chapter about *JFK*—that it is, in its way, as much a Vietnam film as the trilogy of movies that Stone made about the war itself and its immediate aftermath for Vietnamese and Americans alike—is no less true of *Nixon*. Not only does the Vietnam War dominate the Nixon presidency: The Vietnam War both creates and destroys it. While Nixon saw that Kennedy would be unbeatable in 1964 (as Johnson, in the event, actually was), the political situation in 1968 is very different. Johnson's massive escalation and Americanization of the war have split his party into two ferociously opposed prowar and antiwar wings, and it is difficult to see how a party so divided against itself can mount a successful presidential campaign: "The war's crippled the Democrats," as Dick says to Pat, explaining why he must break his earlier promise to her and get back into politics. When Robert Kennedy— the only Democrat who still might conceivably have put together a winning presidential coalition, and whom Nixon deeply fears, largely because of RFK's central role in his brother's campaign eight years earlier—is shot down in a Los Angeles hotel kitchen in June 1968, the path to the White House is clear for Nixon. Haldeman's prophecy to his boss—"Vietnam's gonna put you in there, chief!"—comes perfectly true.

Yet what the war can give it can also—in an irony worthy of Sophoclean or Shakespearian tragedy—take away. The most triumphal scene for Nixon in the entire film is the representation of the 1968 Republican Convention. As he surveys the vast throngs from the stage, thousands of Republicans are wildly cheering their new nominee; Dick and Pat smile at one another like young lovers; a laughing and smiling Haldeman looks happier than we ever see him before or after; and Murray Chotiner and Herb Klein are embracing like old friends reunited. Then Nixon gives his acceptance speech—historically, one of the best rhetorical performances of his entire career and delivered here by Hopkins perhaps even better than the real-life Nixon did it. Though technically Nixon is now only the Republican nominee, we know that, owing to the shambles in which the Democratic Party finds itself, the nomination is tantamount to the presidency itself.

But this jubilant scene is immediately followed by a shot of an antiwar demonstration, with protestors shouting, "The whole world is watching," and then by a slide that informs us that during 1969-1970—well into the Nixon presidency, of course—about 245,000 secret bombings were carried out by US forces in Laos and Cambodia. The war that disabled and ultimately destroyed the Johnson presidency is now consuming Nixon's own. The scene switches to the White House, where the president and his top foreign-policy advisers are discussing the American ground invasion of Cambodia that will take place in April 1970. Secretary of State William Rogers (James Karen) and Secretary of Defense Melvin Laird (Richard Fancy) argue against the move and for some measure of restraint—a representation that accords well with the historical record—but Nixon contemptuously overrules them and, with Kissinger's enthusiastic support, decides in favor of extending and intensifying the war. We see terrifying (and evidently archival) footage of the military action, with an emphasis on vast explosions devastating the Asian countryside. The results at home are what the viewer knows they will be: massive antiwar demonstrations, the killing by the authorities of six unarmed protestors at Kent State and Jackson State, and, in response, the only nationwide student strike in US history.

We next see the president and his closest aides having dinner aboard the White House yacht, and at this point they are deeply rattled by the severity of the crisis—though, characteristically, they see the problem simply in partisan electoral terms. "Jesus Christ, dead kids," says Nixon. "How the hell did we give the Democrats a weapon like this?" "Kent State is not good," agrees Haldeman, and John Ehrlichman (J. T. Walsh), the top White House adviser on domestic affairs, argues that the cost of continuing to prosecute the war will likely be a one-term presidency for Nixon. Nixon muses that perhaps the best solution is to drop nuclear weapons on Vietnam—an idea that evokes sympathy from no one except Kissinger.

And so it goes throughout the film. Seldom does much screen time pass before we are reminded once again of the war's effects both in Vietnam and at home. The persistent footage of bombing and shooting, and of the dead and maimed, remind us that among the victims are not only Mao's "millions of Vietnamese" but also nearly sixty thousand dead Americans, one of whom could easily have been the young volunteer combat infantryman Oliver Stone himself (who in fact was wounded twice in action and received a Purple Heart and a Bronze Star for extraordinary bravery under fire). The film also shows us, again and again, the large antiwar demonstrations that exemplify the way the war is tearing apart the fabric of American society, sometimes, as at Jackson State and Kent State, in literally lethal ways. However much one may admire Nixon's technical skill in dealing with Mao and Brezhnev, it is difficult to see how any such diplomatic nimbleness can truly compensate for the overwhelming horror of the Vietnam War. The Vietnam War is, for Stone, the evil heart of darkness at the center of the Nixon Administration—to borrow the title of the Joseph Conrad novella that inspired Francis Ford Coppola to make perhaps the only American film about Vietnam comparable in importance to Stone's own Vietnam trilogy. If Stone's ultimate claim for John Kennedy in *JFK* is that, but for the bullets of Dealey Plaza, America would have avoided the Vietnam War, his ultimate indictment of Richard Nixon is that, for four long years, Nixon expanded and intensified the senseless slaughter that he inherited from Lyndon Johnson. In precisely sadomasochistic fashion, the war that devastates so many Vietnamese and Americans indirectly devastates the Nixon presidency and so the person of Nixon himself. In good accord with the views of virtually all historians, the film shows how the domestic political crises precipitated by the war (such as those at issue in the scene on the presidential yacht discussed above) led to the White House crimes and dirty tricks known collectively as Watergate—which in turn destroyed the Nixon presidency. It is a nexus that Nixon himself identifies in conversation with Kissinger and with Alexander Haig (Powers Boothe), his final chief of staff, during his last evening in the White House. Attributing his downfall to getting soft and emitting the "rusty, metallic smell" of blood, he says of the smell, "It came over from Vietnam."

If the Vietnam War is Nixon's geopolitical heart of darkness, it cannot, however, be completely understood apart from the more personal darkness in the president's own heart: for, as we have noticed, the dialectic of sadomasochism is inextricable from a specifically Nixonian dialectic of the political and the personal. Stone's Nixon is a profoundly dark figure, and in many ways. In one scene, John Dean, while still loyally working for the president, meets at night, under cover of darkness, with the Watergate burglar E. Howard Hunt (Ed Harris), who is blackmailing Nixon. Dean hopes to persuade—or intimidate—Hunt into ceasing to demand money from the White House in exchange for his silence about Watergate matters, or at least to make clear exactly how much money he intends to demand *in toto*. Hunt is un-intimidated and un-cooperative. But, even more, he is bemused at what he takes to be Dean's innocence about the man for whom he is working; and he is moved to deliver one of the film's definitive judgments on Nixon. "John," he says, "sooner or later—sooner, I think—you're going to learn the lesson that's been learned by everyone who's ever gotten close to Richard Nixon: that he's the darkness reaching out for the darkness." Hunt, whose pity for the young White House counsel's *naïveté* seems somewhat genuine, wanders off into the night, warning Dean, "Your grave's already been dug, John." The footage of the conversation between the two men is intercut with shots of Nixon sitting by himself in—where else?—the dark.

Hunt's—and the film's—insight is ratified by the film's cinematography as well as by its narrative and dramatic aspects. Few predominantly color movies have ever given us so much blackness to look at. Influenced by the black-and-white achievements of German Expressionism and American *film noir* (both genres remote, in most ways, from the tradition of the biopic or film biography that supplies one generic element of Stone's movie), the world of *Nixon* is visually one of darkness and shadow, especially insofar as its protagonist is concerned. When, for instance, we first set eyes on Nixon—after following Alexander Haig through the White House gates and, in a complex series of tracking shots, into the president's inner sanctum—we find Nixon sitting alone, drinking whisky, in a dark room illuminated only by the dim, flickering light of a wood fire. When Haig, after asking permission, turns on an electric lamp, Nixon winces and shades his eyes like Count Dracula assaulted by a ray of sunshine. At this point, Nixon appears almost *literally* to be, as Hunt would say, the darkness reaching out for the darkness.

Later the film achieves a similar but even more remarkable visual effect. In one of the most notable instances of the film's use of complexly shifting temporalities (a technique partly inherited from *Citizen Kane*), a flashback scene from Nixon's earlier life—specifically, from the period of his young manhood when he is played by David Barry Gray—is concerned with his brother Harold's death from tuberculosis and its immediate aftermath. It is of course an event of unspeakable sadness for the Nixon family, yet one that—as Harold himself points out shortly before dying and as Hannah Nixon insists afterwards—may yield some good: namely, that the Nixon family, relieved of the financial burden imposed by the expensive Arizona sanatorium in which Harold was being treated, will now be able to afford to send Richard to law school. The scene ends with a close-up of Gray's handsome face wracked by grief and sympathy but also with some measure of the determination that his mother demands of him. There is then a fade-out from Gray, then a completely black screen, and then a fade-in to a close-up of Anthony Hopkins as the middle-aged Nixon—his face not particularly handsome and marked by no trace of sympathy though perhaps displaying some obscure grief. He is standing alone against a totally black background. His expression is grim, and his eyes dart around with paranoid watchfulness. This is, expressly, Nixon as a creature of the dark. A few moments pass before the viewer is allowed to realize that this is, however, the triumphant scene of the 1968 Republican National Convention, with Nixon about to give his speech accepting the nomination for president. The screen behind Nixon brightens and a band playing "The Battle Hymn of the Republic" is heard, alerting the viewer to where we are. Hopkins looks around as though he, like us, has just realized where he is, and then flashes a precise duplicate of the real-life Nixon's weirdly mechanical smile. The point is vividly made that the darkness is Nixon's "natural" home, from which he emerges only for specifically calculated reasons.

So complicated, however, is Nixon's character as Stone constructs it that the darkness in which he dwells does not invariably connote only the kind of pure evil that Hunt presumably means—or, indeed, the kind of pure evil exemplified by Richard Helms, or by Clay Shaw and his fellow conspirators in *JFK*. With darkness, sometimes, can come insight. A pertinent scene in this regard is based on one of the weirdest real-life episodes of the Nixon presidency: his late-night visit to the Lincoln Memorial to chat with some of the anti-war protestors who were all over central Washington in the days following the Cambodian invasion and the killings at Kent State and Jackson State. In the film, Nixon slips out of the White House at 4:00 a.m. under cover of night, leaving his entire staff and his Secret Service guards behind, and accompanied only by his personal body servant Manolo (Tony Plana). He arrives at the Memorial to find it bathed in the darkness of night, though the giant statue of Lincoln radiates preternatural brightness (presumably meant to suggest Lincoln's status as Nixon's ultimate hero). Most of the demonstrators are asleep all over the place on blankets and in sleeping bags, but a small crowd of them gathers at his arrival, astonished to see the man against whom they are protesting actually in their midst. Nixon seems genuinely interested in conversing with the protestors, but most of the back-and-forth talk runs, initially, along all too predictable lines: the protestors insisting that the war must end at once, Nixon replying that he too desires peace, but a peace with honor that cannot necessarily be achieved right away. Nixon also makes some awkward attempts at humor (this is where he says that he was used as a tackling dummy during his college football career).

Things take a more interesting turn, however, when a fiercely articulate nineteen-year-old woman (Joanna Going) comes to a sudden insight while she is arguing with the president: "You can't stop it [the war], can you? Even if you wanted to. Because it's not you, it's the system." Nixon has been able to parry, with the ease of a skilled and experienced politician, the demonstrators' more conventional antiwar assertions, which have assumed him to be the main evil force behind the Vietnam War. But the woman's words strike him deeply: as is indicated by intercut black-and-white shots of the darkest moments in his own personal history, the deaths by tuberculosis of Harold and also of his younger brother Arthur (Joshua Preston). The woman says that Nixon is "powerless," and he hotly denies it, the pain in his voice perhaps at least partly based on remembering that his brothers—and his entire family—were powerless against the disease. In a tone that suggests he is trying to convince himself as much as the young woman with whom he is debating, Nixon insists, "Because I understand the system, I believe I can control it—maybe not control it totally, but tame it enough to make it do some good." "Sounds like you're talking about a wild animal," the woman replies. "Yeah, maybe I am," Nixon agrees. A few minutes later, he muses to Haldeman—who has arrived with other staffers and with the Secret Service to bring the president back from his strange adventure—that, remarkably, this college kid understands, at the age of nineteen, something that it has taken him 25 years in politics to grasp: that the American power structure, consisting of, for example, "the CIA, the Mafia, those Wall Street bastards," is a wild animal, a "beast" as he puts it. It should be remembered that this is the exact same term we will later hear him use to describe the secret government that killed Kennedy. There immediately follows a somewhat surreal montage that most prominently includes shots of the Vietnam War and the John Kennedy assassination.

It will be recalled that the beast that killed Kennedy is referred to by Nixon as something that "we" created. Nixon is a creature of the darkness, but he never feels completely at home there, and so is sometimes able to contemplate it with the shrewd perspective of the outsider, or semi-outsider. He is part of the secret government, of the beast, in the sense that he has been involved with

Black Ops since his years as Ike's vice-president. Yet, with his lower-middle-class resentment of "the elite," he feels alienated from the beast too: whether he is being bullied by the cool, elegant Helms in the director's private CIA office, or remembering how (as we have heard him complain) "those Wall Street bastards" refused to give him a job in any of their white-shoe law firms when he graduated from Duke. Despite being situated in the heart of darkness—or rather, in some ways, precisely because of it—Nixon can, as he puts it, "understand the system" and sometimes see beyond it.

There are, indeed, occasional glimmers of a different Nixon *in potentia*, one who might have opposed the power structure that he has, in actuality, devoted his life to serving ("Billionaires Rule, Nixon's Their Tool," as one antiwar banner puts it). One example is the conversation with the never-named young woman at the Lincoln Memorial played by Joanna Going. Another, even more explicit example comes in a scene of another massive antiwar demonstration, one about a year later. As Nixon, in the company of J. Edgar Hoover (Bob Hoskins), gazes from a White House window at a throng of perhaps a quarter million protestors, he feels a flicker of sympathy for those who have come to Washington to oppose his war policy. He muses to the FBI director, "You think they got a point, Edgar? This whole damn system of government." Hoover, of course, does not think that they have a point—he bizarrely compares the current situation in the United States to that in Russia just before Lenin and the Bolsheviks took power in 1917—and Nixon quickly drops this line of thought. Yet it is clear that, in his tragic complexity, he is a different sort of person from Hoover (or Helms).

Nixon: American Tragedy

The national tragedy of *Nixon* is also a specifically *American* tragedy. What is at stake here is most obviously the tragedy of what

Nixon does to America: above all, of course, the Vietnam War, though, as Stone's *Heaven & Earth* (1993) makes even clearer than *Nixon* does, the devastation that the war inflicted on Vietnam was infinitely worse. But what is also of fundamental importance is the distinctly American form that Nixon's own tragedy takes. Here again the impact on Stone of *Citizen Kane* is relevant, for Welles's film is perhaps the most quintessentially American of all great cinematic tragedies. Its Americanness is suggested in the very name of the movie, whose significance has not, in general, been sufficiently appreciated: for the point is surely that, in a republic like the United States, whose constitution explicitly prohibits titles of nobility, "citizen" is the loftiest designation that anyone can enjoy. It is no accident that, when we see Charles Foster Kane at his youngest, as a little boy playing in the Colorado snow, the words we hear him casually singing to himself are, "The Union forever!"—the utterance taken from the lyrics of "Battle Cry of Freedom" (1862), an extremely popular Civil War song that celebrates the endurance and triumph of the unified American nation. Later, as a middle-aged newspaper magnate of huge wealth and influence, Kane conveys much the same sentiment with full intent. As we noted in the preceding chapter, Kane is at one point described (by a Wall Street financier) as a communist and at another (by a labor leader) as a fascist. His effective reply to all such charges is decisive: "I am, have been, and will be only one thing—an American." Kane is fully and proudly aware that the story Welles presents is one that could unfold only in America.

The same is true of the story that Stone tells in *Nixon*; and his film is just as self-conscious of its Americanness as its Wellesian precursor. Perhaps the most unexpected scene in the entire three and a half hours of *Nixon* is the very first one. It is a black-and-white movie-within-the-movie that seems to be a training film for salesmen; it features an older and apparently more accomplished salesman giving advice to a younger one whose career is in trouble. "A good salesman can sell anything," the mentor advises. But he also warns, "You have to remember what you're *really* selling—yourself." It turns out that this seemingly unremarkable piece of celluloid is being played in a hotel conference room where the Watergate burglars are relaxing over drinks immediately prior to breaking into the offices of the Democratic National Committee. Though the content of the film is on the diegetic level purely contingent (in historical fact, the burglars played a film in order to drown out conversation about the crime that they were preparing to commit), it is not by carelessness that this short embedded film is the first thing Stone gives the viewer to look at.

For the training film announces (perhaps with a deliberate nod to *Death of a Salesman*, arguably the most typical and enduring of all American stage tragedies)[57] the form of American identity and American ambition that will define the Nixon of the film, whom the viewer at this point has yet to see. It is not the hearty, confident ambition of a Charles Foster Kane, who from childhood has enjoyed vast wealth and privilege. Instead, it is the brittle, insecure ambition of the petty-bourgeois striver desperately attempting to better himself in the snake pit of a highly competitive society. The salesman represents—as is shown by Arthur Miller (and by his follower David Mamet in *Glengarry Glen Ross* [1984], another major American tragedy)—the purest instance of this quintessentially American pattern. But an electoral politician is, of course, a salesman too, and one who not only sells himself but is constantly selling *nothing but* himself. This is especially true of a politician like Nixon, who, unlike Jack Kennedy, begins with no inherited fortune or network of social and political connections, and must therefore depend upon his own efforts at self-promotion for everything. The sadomasochistic pre-occupation with himself that Stone's Nixon so consistently displays is thus by no means an outlook chosen quite freely. But nor is it one forced upon Nixon *only* by his relentlessly moralistic upbringing and his resulting mother-complex.

It is also integral to his entire social and national situation as an American.

Stone's Nixon is not only as fully aware of his Americanness as Welles's Kane. Like Kane, though in a rather different way, he also takes tremendous pride in his national identity. A pertinent sequence in this regard begins with one of the film's more surreal scenes. Nixon gives a White House news conference in January 1973 to announce that he has arranged a peace accord in Vietnam that will result in a cessation of fighting and the return of America's prisoners of war. Expecting to be lauded as a hero, he is in fact met with a barrage of unrelieved hostility from the assembled journalists. One reporter points out that Nixon's accord could have been reached four years earlier when he first assumed the presidency; the four years of sometimes intensified and always unspeakably destructive warfare were pointless. Other reporters pepper him with extremely unwelcome questions about Watergate. The scene is surreal in the sense that the White House press corps never actually behaved even remotely like that during the Nixon Administration; on the contrary, until the final days of Watergate, Nixon enjoyed generally quite favorable treatment from America's journalists.[58] The scene must be understood subjectively, as representing the way that Nixon *feels* himself always to be under attack by the nation's "elite," a grouping in which he most definitely includes the press. As at numerous other points in the film (for instance, the journalistic description noted above of the Christmas 1972 bombing as "without doubt the most brutal bombing in American history," a phrase uttered with the generic American accent and the tone of self-satisfied authority characteristic of "objective" journalism in the United States, but which no real-life journalist would have ever actually used outside of the most marginalized forums of the hard left), the portrayal of press coverage of Nixon is designed less to dramatize historical reality than to show Nixon's masochistic sense of being assailed and violated.

Predictably, Nixon's masochistic experience of the press conference is immediately followed by a series of sadistic outbursts. Departing from the briefing room, he expresses his frustration with the journalists by giving his press secretary Ron Ziegler (David Paymer) a viciously hard shove. Alone in a private White House room with Haldeman and other close aides, he starts throwing things against the wall. He bizarrely rants that Edward Kennedy is somehow behind the journalists' savaging of him—the Kennedys always and inevitably the central object of *ressentiment* in the Nixonian imagination—and that he is being persecuted because of his physical appearance and his educational background (Whittier College rather than Harvard, presumably). But, when he asks why his enemies hate him, it is Haldeman who supplies the answer that his boss really wants: "Because they're not Americans." Nixon instantly and emphatically agrees: "That's right, they don't trust America." To say that the president's (American) opponents are "not Americans" is, strictly speaking, a meaningless contradiction in terms. But Haldeman knows what his boss means, and proceeds to explain the matter in precisely the terms that Nixon desires:

Why would they [trust America]? They just come here to stick their snouts in the trough. Who are these people? Sulzberger [presumably Arthur Ochs "Punch" Sulzberger, at that time the publisher of *The New York Times*]. Their parents are gold traders from eastern Europe; [to Kissinger] with all due respect, Henry. They buy things. They come here to Jew York City [*sic*] and buy up things. And one of the things they buy, Mr. President, is *The New York Times*. You know what? You should be proud, because they'll never trust you, sir. Because we speak for the average American.

Charles Foster Kane (who himself bought many things in New York City, and elsewhere) would not have disagreed—though he would never have felt the need to describe his own American identity in such defensive and sadistic terms.

The notion that some Americans are more American or more "really" American than others can be license for the most virulent forms of bigotry—as Haldeman's anti-Semitic rant illustrates plainly enough. Yet that is not the whole story. From the opening black-and-white film-within-the-film, Stone, like Arthur Miller and David Mamet and many other American artists before him, suggests, as we have seen, that America is, at some fundamental level, a nation of salesmen: a nation of insecure middle-class and lower-middle-class aspirants to success who have inherited nothing of value and must constantly and sleeplessly compete in a cutthroat arena where most competitors are bound to lose, and where even the winners of today may well be the losers of tomorrow or the day after. In this sense, Stone's Nixon is indeed as quintessentially American as he and Haldeman maintain. To have enjoyed some success on these terms—to be a "self-made man"—is a familiar and deeply American boast; and Nixon (unlike Kane) often reminds us that he has worked hard for everything he has.[59]

Yet the American—including the Nixonian—imagination has always been haunted by the suspicion that there is an aesthetically finer and more satisfying way to live than this incessant American self-making: a way of which the United States has been largely deprived by its history as a middle-class country from the beginning, and one therefore lacking the inherited upper-class polish and aristocratic culture of old Europe. In modern America, the quasi-aristocratic Kennedys are easily understood as providing the closest thing the nation has had to royalty at its most appealing: and, among the Kennedys, most especially John Fitzgerald Kennedy of Camelot. This is the deepest significance of Norman Mailer's image (referred to in a note to the previous chapter) of JFK as Superman come to the supermarket. If there is something "un-American" about this kind of glamor, Nixon's bitter resentment of it is—like all resentment, according to Nietzsche—inextricably bound up with immense (and, in this case, perfectly American) envy and repressed admiration. Perhaps the most profound line of dialogue in the entirety of *Nixon* comes toward the end, as Nixon, wandering the White House by himself during his final night as its occupant, looks up at the official portrait of John Kennedy and addresses his dead rival and predecessor with an observation about their fellow Americans: "When they look at you, they see what they want to be. When they look at me, they see what they are." On one level, this is the ultimate message of the film itself; and it is not accidental that, shortly thereafter, the final credits are presented over a lovely choral rendition of "Shenandoah"—as archetypically American a song as has ever been composed.

Conclusion

But "Shenandoah" is an expression of irredeemable American *loss*. So, finally, is the entire duology composed of *JFK* and *Nixon*. As different as the two films are, one of the many things that unites them is that both leave the viewer with unspeakable sadness at the state of the American union. Though only *Nixon* is a tragedy in the true generic sense, the Kennedy assassination at the heart of *JFK* is certainly, for Stone, "tragic" in the more colloquial meaning of a terrible, disastrous event. As we have discussed, the earlier film assumes that the rifles of Dealey Plaza not only cut down a particular charismatic leader but cancelled JFK's plans to withdraw US troops from Vietnam and, more generally, to liquidate the Cold War and to replace armed opposition between the US and the USSR with peaceful competition in economic, scientific, cultural, and other endeavors. The immediate result was the horror of the Vietnam War.

In its vision of American loss, the later film is, as ever, more complex. On one level the disaster is the Nixon Administration itself—primarily the continuation, intensification, and expansion of the war inherited from Lyndon Johnson, but also (a matter rarely foregrounded in the film but not ignored altogether) the white racist demagogy historically so essential to Nixon's capture of the White House in the first place. Yet the film suggests that, if Nixon's accession to the presidency was a terrible thing for the country, so, perhaps, in some ways, was his forced resignation of the office. The complex irony characteristic of tragedy would in this way be complete. However brutal his war policy had been, US combat troops had, after all, been withdrawn from Vietnam by the time that Nixon left the White House. Looking back with knowledge of the Reaganite foreign and military policy to come, the film, as we have considered above, allows that there was perhaps something to be said for the rough state of equilibrium among the planet's three largest powers that Nixon seemed to be establishing: what Nixon, in the conversation onboard the White House yacht, calls "triangular diplomacy," which Kissinger explains as "the linking of the whole world for self-interest." Considering the two movies of the duology together, one might almost argue that, with the opening to China and the détente with the Soviet Union, Nixon briefly accomplished a (much) milder version of what JFK was murdered for merely planning.

It remains to examine how the agential status of the two men identified by the movies' titles operates in the duology's vision of American loss and American history. As with *Richard III* or *Henry V*, the titles imply a large role for the named individuals; and the prominence granted an American president in our time may seem as unexceptionable as that granted an English king in Shakespeare's. But precisely what kind of function do individuals, even the most powerful, play in the historical process? This is, of course, a perennial question in the philosophy of history, and virtually every conceivable answer to it has been argued at one time or another. At one extreme, there is the view that history is made by "great men" (or, rarely, great women), who are capable of bending events to their will. This is the heroic interpretation of history, whose most canonical exponent remains, probably, Thomas Carlyle, with his widely quoted encapsulations of this view: "Universal History, the history of what man has accomplished in this world, is at bottom the History of the Great Men who have worked here"—and, even more succinctly, "The History of the world is but the Biography of great men."[60] At the opposed extreme, there is the Tolstoyan position that history is made by large transpersonal forces that the individual can barely even understand, let along control. According to this view, those whom the hero-worshippers call great (paradigmatically Napoleon Bonaparte for Tolstoy himself) are actually the slaves, not the masters, of the historical process. (It is perhaps worth mentioning that, though the real-life Nixon's voracious reading was almost entirely nonfiction, Tolstoy was one of the very few novelists that interested him.) Of course, there are many more complex views as well of the individual in history; and there are doubtless elements even in Carlyle and Tolstoy themselves that suggest greater complexity than these extremely brief summaries allow. But all such more complex perspectives tend to be either compromises between, or dialectical sublimations of, the starkly opposed positions outlined here.

Stone's Kennedy/Nixon duology provides a good deal of material for thought about this question of historical agency without ever deciding flatly for either the Tolstoyan or the Carlylian view. Once again, *JFK* is the simpler of the two films. Given the premise that Kennedy was murdered in a Black Op by the secret, permanent government because of his determination to end the Cold War, an obvious question, which the film never answers unambiguously, is just this: *Could* JFK have succeeded? Here certain different elements of the movie are somewhat at odds with one another. The hero-worshipping, perhaps virtually Carlylian, view of JFK on which the film is largely based tends to cut against the notion that his final political project was doomed from the start. Many, to be sure, would insist emphatically that lost causes can be heroic. But to *initiate* a struggle that one ought to know in advance is certain to be lost appears less heroic than pathetic—and pathos is clearly *not* the dominant quality in the way that the film wants to portray President Kennedy. Much the same is true of Kennedy's avenger and symbolic son, Jim Garrison. His project—to expose JFK's killers—is far more modest than JFK's own but exactly congruent with it politically; and it also fails. Garrison is unable to put together a legally convincing case even against the single defendant Clay Shaw, let alone any of Shaw's superiors in the conspiracy—none of whom Garrison is ever even able to name. Yet at the end Garrison's head, though as bloodied metaphorically as Kennedy's has been literally, is unbowed. He vows to fight on, to continue on the trail of the assassins for as long as the job takes. The melodramatic ethical structure of *JFK*, in which Kennedy and Garrison are paladins of righteousness, fighting against the forces of darkness, impels us to see the struggles that these heroes undertake not as mere hopeless fiascos but as noble failures that might have succeeded.

Yet the film's view of the secret government constituted by America's national-security state makes it difficult to see just *how* Kennedy or Garrison could have succeeded. It is not only that the conspiracy to kill Kennedy appears to have been organized at the highest levels of the Pentagon and the CIA—that is, by the men with the guns, who on any purely political level are, almost by definition, the supreme power in any society ("Political power grows out of the barrel of a gun," as Mao famously put it). The point is also that these men are backed by, and in the last analysis function in the service of, vast amounts of capital—as "X" makes clear in the tutorial he gives to Garrison, where he effectively echoes the remarks about the military-industrial complex in Eisenhower's farewell speech that the film has highlighted at its beginning. Furthermore, the fact that the conspiracy is glimpsed in only the most fragmentary and fleeting way makes it seem, as we discussed above, all the more frightening and, in a closely related effect, all the more omnicompetent. We see almost nothing of the actual mechanisms by which the secret government works but are never in doubt that work it does. Exactly how, for example, do the real conspirators assure the cooperation of much less powerful but structurally key organizations like the Dallas Police Department—without, presumably, the latter ever really knowing what is going on? We cannot say, though there is little question but that such cooperation is indeed accomplished. When the secret government is seen in this way, any merely presidential action against its essential functions does indeed seem hopeless; and, of course, the powers that can murder their own nominal commander-in-chief would have little trouble in thwarting the investigative efforts of an underfunded local district attorney.

So *JFK* maintains a rather delicate balance as to what degree agency lies with heroic individuals and to what degree with larger and transpersonal forces. The same is true, though in a (predictably) more complicated way, of *Nixon*. The antiwar protestor played by Joanna Going gives explicit voice to an anti-heroic and deterministic view—"[I]t's not you, it's the system"—that, as we have seen, is, at least to some degree, endorsed not only by the film but by Nixon himself. (One may wonder whether the insomniac president had perhaps been rereading *War and Peace* [1869].) The young woman's insight is one that more generally haunts both *Nixon* and Nixon. Once again we should recall the crucial scene in Richard Helms's office. If President Nixon acknowledges Helms and Hoover as the only two Americans perhaps more knowledgeable and more politically powerful than himself, it is not primarily because of any remarkable personal qualities intrinsic to the men themselves. The impeccably groomed, unflappable, tennis-playing, flower-tending, Yeats-quoting patrician Helms seems a fairly conventional specimen of the "elite" that Nixon so abhors, and one without the public charisma or the magnetic personal attractiveness of a Jack Kennedy.

Hoover—who, when not present, is contemptuously described by Nixon as "that little closet fairy" and, after his death, as "the little shit," "the old queen," and "that old cocksucker"—is portrayed as a sexual predator with the manners of a stereotypical desk sergeant and the morals of a Mafia extortionist. What makes Helms and Hoover so supremely formidable is not any personal heroism on their part but the fact that they function as the personifications of the CIA and the FBI, respectively: that is, of two agencies ("agencies" in both the bureaucratic and the philosophical senses of the word) absolutely integral to the secret government. It is the "system," as the young woman says, or the "beast," as Nixon himself says, that confronts Nixon with an ability to influence events that may baffle even that of the presidency itself.

Yet at this point we should engage a hypothesis about the secret government that is *absent* from Stone's movie. Those who have sneered at the filmmaker as a "conspiracy theorist" should notice that he ignores a fascinating and by no means implausible conspiracy theory that in some ways could have fit into his film extremely well. We know that the White House tapes were the instrument that made Nixon's political self-destruction all but inevitable, and that their existence was made known to the Ervin Committee and then to the world at large by Haldeman's aide Alexander Butterfield. We also know that, as noted above, there have long been rumors that Butterfield was a CIA mole—that, while officially working for Haldeman and Nixon, Butterfield was secretly working for and reporting back to Helms. No real proof for this connection between Helms and Butterfield has ever been produced, and Helms himself tersely (and, of course, unsurprisingly) denied it.[61] But it makes a certain amount of sense. Presumably any CIA director has reason to keep tabs on the president of the moment, especially one whose relations with the Agency were as fraught and uncertain as Nixon's; and Butterfield, who worked in closer daily proximity to Nixon than any other White House aide except Haldeman, could have very efficiently served as Helms's plant. Furthermore, Helms, as a career CIA man with, presumably, a strong sense of loyalty to the organization, would have had good reason to be outraged by Nixon's attempt to use the CIA and besmirch its name in order to cover his own criminal tracks after the Watergate burglaries. The hypothesis, then, that Helms destroyed Nixon's presidency by ordering Butterfield to reveal the existence of the tapes could have worked quite cogently in Stone's *Nixon*. It would have enacted Nixon's defeat at the hands of "the beast," and it would even have made for a neat parallelism between the two halves of the duology, with the two very different downfalls of the two very different presidents both engineered by the same most secret component of the secret government, in both cases incarnate in the person of Richard Helms. It will be recalled that, in the scene in *Nixon* in Helms's office, the director all but openly acknowledges his part in the JFK assassination.

Yet, in fact, the putative Helms-Butterfield connection never appears in Stone's movie. The closest we ever come to it is a remark by J. Edgar Hoover, in which the FBI director informs Nixon that Helms has placed CIA operatives all over the White House; but he does not identify any of them by name. Of course, it may be that Oliver Stone has found the possibility of collusion between Helms and Butterfield to be unconvincing, or even (though this seems less plausible) uninteresting. (It is perhaps worth noting that Butterfield is credited as a "technical consultant" on *Nixon*.) But, whatever the filmmaker's personal intentions may have been, there are deeper generic reasons to have foregone use of a Helms-Butterfield plot as the engine of Nixon's political destruction. Such use would have made *Nixon* too deterministic and anti-heroic, and would have somewhat flattened out the tragic depth of the film. Though the system, the "beast," may possess a power greater than that of any White House, Stone's Nixon is not to be seen purely as a victim of the endless malevolence of the secret government—as

Stone's Kennedy is. Unlike JFK, Nixon has his own part to play in his tragic catastrophe.

Indeed, the film's refusal to choose decisively between the heroic and the deterministic views of history—between Carlyle and Tolstoy, as it were—is what enables, on the philosophical level, the construction of Nixon as a tragic hero-villain in the precise Aristotelian sense of one who is neither completely innocent of, nor completely responsible for, his own destruction. Nixon has some real agency in his own downfall and symbolic death: but also, it is fair to note, in the more positive aspects of his heroic identity. When Dick says to Pat, referring to the 180-degree turn that he has engineered in US policy toward the People's Republic of China, "Only Nixon could have done that," the self-hero-worship is doubtless not to be taken entirely at face value. Not only does the statement seem to deny Kissinger the share of the credit that Nixon is at other times willing to grant him, but it also ignores the way that (as Nixon is perfectly aware) the opening to China is driven by the more fundamental transpersonal antagonism between the United States and the Soviet Union. Still, the film does not suggest that the diplomatic move was inevitable, and it clearly shows the importance of Nixon's geopolitical insight and deftness in playing the China card. Nixon, indeed, may have been uniquely qualified to do so: For, as Nixon and Haldeman discuss in the scene on the White House yacht, it was Nixon's old record of ferociously right-wing anti-communism that enabled him to go to what American politicians had generally called "Red China" without facing the domestic political firestorm that would likely have destroyed a liberal Democrat who attempted the same thing. In that sense, perhaps only Nixon could have done it indeed.

But it is, of course, in the catastrophe of the tragedy that Nixon's agency is most prominent. The sadomasochism that so largely defines his character—formed, as the scene of the corn-silk cigarette shows it, *literally* at his mother's knee—leads with perfect appropriateness to the ultimately masochistic act of political self-destruction. Throughout the film, we see this fatal flaw (or mistake) in Nixon expressed in a thousand large and small ways. We see it in the sadism of ordering "the most brutal bombing in American history," and in considering the use of nuclear weapons against Vietnam—a country, it should always be remembered, that had never attacked or even threatened the United States in any way. We see it, too, in the crudely racist and anti-Semitic presidential language found, shockingly even to Nixon himself, on the White House tapes. We see it in Nixon's endless masochistic torturing of himself through his obsession with all the advantages and attractions that life granted to the Kennedys and denied to him. We see it in the excruciatingly complex relation that Nixon bears to the "elite," to the American power structure that he in so many ways detests—whether he is being denied a job by "those Wall Street bastards" or being intimidated by Richard Helms with almost explicit threats of assassination—and yet that he ultimately serves so loyally.

Alone of all the characters in the film, it is Pat Nixon, as the one-woman Greek chorus of the tragedy, who sees, with a clarity that is unbearably painful to her, where the path on which her husband is set is bound to lead. He himself sees it only at the very end. Like Oedipus or Othello or Lear, Nixon, in the moment of absolute disaster, gains an insight he has never attained before. As in the Sophoclean and Shakespearian examples, the perspective of the protagonist is finally fused with that of the audience. In addition, actual history is seamlessly joined to cinematic representation as Anthony Hopkins voices the most pregnant lines of the farewell address to his staff that the real-life Nixon delivered on his last morning in the White House: "Always remember: others may hate you. But those who hate you don't win—unless you hate them. And then, you destroy yourself." It is often the privilege of the tragic protagonist to depart at the height of eloquence: "The rest is silence"—"And say besides, that in Aleppo once. . . ."—"Thou'lt come no more/Never, never, never, never, never!"—"I/Flutter'd your Volscians in Corioli;/Alone I did it!" In joining the company of Hamlet, Othello, Lear, and Coriolanus, Stone's Nixon could reflect that he thus gains a particular kind of luster denied to John Kennedy.[62]

CHAPTER III

Bush: (Un)Fortunate Son

Bush: (Un)Fortunate Son

From Tragedy to Farce

The opening lines of *The Eighteenth Brumaire of Louis Bonaparte* (1852) have been quoted so many times—not to mention adapted, paraphrased, parodied, and referred to in almost every other conceivable way—that one may hesitate to invoke them once again. But, of course, the main reason that Marx's words have proved so memorable is that they really do apply to so many different historical and cultural situations: "Hegel remarks somewhere that all the great events and characters of world history occur, so to speak, twice. He forgot to add: the first time as tragedy, the second as farce."[63] As we have seen, not only is *Nixon* a tragedy in the strict generic sense, but Stone's entire Kennedy/Nixon duology is tragic in the looser colloquial meaning, directing our attention to the unspeakable horror and disaster of the Vietnam War. As Garrison leaves the courtroom at the end of the first installment of the duology, and as Nixon prepares to leave the White House at the end of the second, it is clear that the state of the American union is one that can only inspire profound sadness, though a sadness that, as in all tragedy, is not without an element of grandeur.

Whether or not the historical moment of George W. Bush is to be considered farcical in comparison to the moment of Kennedy and

Nixon—a matter to which we will return—there is no doubt that Stone's *W.* (2008) has important generic elements of comedy and farce: thus sharply distinguishing the film from the high seriousness of the duology, neither half of which can boast, among many and various merits, anything much in the way of humor (except perhaps a few passages of the darkest conceivable humor in *Nixon*).[64] Made thirteen years after the completion of the Kennedy/Nixon films, *W.* does not speak to the earlier movies to anything like the same degree that they speak to one another. It would thus be inappropriate to consider the three films a trilogy. Still, *W.* does establish some semantic and historical relationships with its predecessors, as, indeed, is suggested by the mere fact that, like them, it focuses on an American president named by the title. *W.* implicitly presents itself as (*inter alia*) a comic—or, perhaps better, a semi-comic, or, best of all, a seriocomic—sequel or spin-off that follows the duology at some distance while maintaining genuine, if often comparatively tenuous, connections to it.

The relative lightness of the film in contrast to the thrilling melodrama of *JFK* and the high neo-Shakespearian tragedy of *Nixon* is signaled in the very title. Whereas Kennedy is named by the initials that he himself chose for an appellation (in large part, no doubt, in order to remind Americans of Franklin D. Roosevelt, or FDR, who in 1960 remained the all-time political hero for most Democratic voters)[65], and Nixon is identified simply by his surname, George W. Bush is reduced to the smallness of his middle initial. Though "W." (or sometimes "Dubya") became prominent in conventional journalistic discourse partly in order to distinguish George W. Bush from his presidential father, who always designated himself simply as "George Bush," it is nonetheless plain that to call the younger Bush by a single letter is necessarily deflationary and at least vaguely funny.[66] It should be added that *W.* is not only a lighter follower to *JFK* and *Nixon*, but a lesser one as well: lesser at least in the sense that its standard feature-film length (just over two hours) contrasts with the "epic" length of the two earlier movies (in each case roughly three and a half hours)—though also in the sense that few viewers, probably, would rank this skillfully made and entertaining film as quite aesthetically equal to its predecessors.

The comedy of W., like the tragedy of *Nixon*, is located squarely in the person of its central character. Indeed, just as *Nixon* is a more personally focused film than *JFK*, so W. is more personal yet. Bush being far less of a politically absorbed personality than Nixon, W. has more conceptual space to concentrate on more purely individual matters of character.

As a character, George W. Bush is frequently portrayed as a laughable buffoon. The first substantial scene in the film is a White House meeting with Bush (Josh Brolin) and his top subordinates at which preparations for the 2003 invasion of Iraq are being discussed. "Axis of Evil" is being considered as a slogan to designate Iran, Iraq, and North Korea, when the national-security adviser Condoleezza Rice (Thandie Newton) raises an objection. North Korea and Iraq are outright dictatorships, whereas Iran, as Rice points out, has a democratically elected president. "As always, Guru, sharp!" Bush compliments Rice, addressing her, as he frequently addresses each of his aides, with a nickname of his own devising. But he rambles on, "Iran is not Iraq, and Iraq is not Iran; I know that"—sounding rather like a fifth-grader trying to convince himself that he is adequately prepared for a geography quiz—and then muses about the spread of democracy in a way that indicates that he has already forgotten Rice's point completely. The room is full of advisers of considerable knowledge and experience of foreign and military policy— not only Rice, but also Vice-President Dick Cheney (Richard Dreyfuss), Secretary of State Colin Powell (Jeffrey Wright), Secretary of Defense Donald Rumsfeld (Scott Glenn), Deputy Secretary of Defense Paul Wolfowitz (Dennis Boutsikaris), and CIA Director George Tenet (Bruce McGill)—and yet, bizarrely, and almost as in a Bakhtinian carnivalesque farce, the man in command of them all free-associates in self-satisfied ignorance. There is some sense of the world ludicrously turned upside down.

The effect, therefore, is not as jarring as it logically "ought" to be when the film suddenly cuts from enormously consequential war planning at the White House to a grotesquely rowdy initiation ceremony several decades earlier at the "Deke" (Delta Kappa Epsilon) fraternity house at Yale University. The sudden movement from high to low—from a room where powerful men (and one powerful woman) determine geopolitical military action to a room where silly overgrown boys make jackasses of themselves—is deliberately deprived of any completely sharp contrast by the fact that the "highness" of the Bush White House has already been severely undercut by the buffoonery of Bush himself. And so it goes throughout the movie. Though, as we will discuss, the ultimate political focus of W. is on the Iraq War—the most hideously destructive and aggressive war launched by the United States since Vietnam itself—the comical persona of its titular character forecloses the kind of sustained gravitas that dominates the equally war-focused JFK and Nixon.

Thus, for example, during a lunch meeting at the White House between Bush and Cheney tête-à-tête—during which Cheney attempts to persuade Bush of the necessity of invading Iraq, though Bush does not really seem to need much, or perhaps any, persuading—the seriousness of the subject-matter contrasts with the unseriousness of Bush. Brolin's representation of Bush is, in its way, as consummate as Anthony Hopkins's of Nixon; and, like Hopkins's performance, it is a genuinely dramatic incarnation rather than a mere impersonation. In this scene, Brolin gives a brilliantly comical effect to the way that, throughout the conversation, Bush smacks his lips and sticks his fingers in his mouth, and, in general, seems intent less on matters of war and peace than on heartily eating a sandwich and drinking a glass of (apparently) iced tea. At one point in the conversation, Bush, reminding Cheney of their administration's achievements thus far, says, "We've got this Guantanamera open." The ridiculous flub is ideological as well as purely verbal, which is perhaps why Cheney feels the need to correct Bush, offering him the term he presumably meant, "Guantanamo." The president would surely be horrified to know that the popular song "Guantanamera," with lyrics by the Cuban writer, theorist, and independence hero José Martí, has long been a prominent anthem of Fidel Castro's Cuban Revolution and, to some degree, of the Latin American left in general—a point doubtless intended by Oliver Stone, the maker of *Salvador* (1986) and of admiring documentaries about the Cuban Revolution, Hugo Chávez's Bolivarian movement in Venezuela, and other progressive Latin American movements.[67] When Cheney, just before departing, gives Bush an important document to read, the president glances at it and says, "Only three pages—good!". Bush, in actuality the only US president to earn degrees from both Yale and Harvard, seems, here, to find reading a burden; in the film, the main activity that occupies his leisure time is watching football or baseball games on television. Having made the case for war to his own satisfaction, Cheney leaves so that Bush can give his undivided attention to eating a piece of pie for dessert.

Or consider another farcical moment. In their bedroom with his wife Laura (Elizabeth Banks), shortly after his father has been elected president in 1988, Bush is feeling dejected. Karl Rove (Toby Jones), a Bush family political strategist who will ultimately become known as George W. Bush's "brain," has told W. that he possesses considerable natural political talent: but also that, so far, he has no real achievements on the basis of which he could launch a political career. "Rove hit me with a 2-by-4 of truth tonight," Bush tells his wife, and a few moments later goes on, "I mean, who ever remembers the son of a president?" Laura, clearly exasperated and just wanting to get to sleep, offers the example of John Quincy Adams. Her husband seems uncertain of the reference, and replies, "Yeah, but that was like 300 years ago, wasn't it?"—although, of course, the

US presidency itself had at this point existed for only 200 years. Or again: A sequence that depicts Bush's first campaign for governor of Texas in 1994 begins with reporters asking him numerous questions about education that he is unable to answer convincingly or even coherently (or even, sometimes, grammatically). Asked how he thinks student progress should be measured, he replies, "Oh—well, we need to make a wholesale effort against racial profiling, which is illiterate children." He later says that he is opposed to a school system that "suckles" children. Rove is at his wit's end, and seems to fear that the whole campaign may have been a mistake. But he manages to divide all the issues into four "food groups" (crime, education, tort reform, and welfare) and drills into Bush enough rote responses about these matters (as well as about several more personal ones) that the candidate manages to get through the election successfully. Or yet again: Presiding over a White House meeting when it is becoming evident that Saddam Hussein's weapons of mass destruction, which were the ostensible justification for the Iraq invasion, never actually existed, Bush gets increasingly upset and confusedly babbles, "You fool me once, shame on you. Now, fool me twice, and—and—you can't get fooled again."

It may, indeed, be questioned how historically "fair" Stone is being in thus representing Bush as clownishly unable to speak his native language properly. A good deal of ordinary everyday speech contains plenty of verbal misfires that would look or sound ridiculous if reproduced on the page or the screen. The blooper about getting fooled, represented in the film as taking place in a private high-level meeting, is closely based on an actual remark in a public speech that Bush gave in Nashville in 2002. Similarly, one of the things that, in the film, the gubernatorial candidate Bush says to the journalists questioning him about education—"You know, rarely is the question asked, 'Is our children learning'?"—is taken almost verbatim from a speech that the real Bush gave in South Carolina two years earlier. But politicians, especially those as loquacious as

Bush, talk a huge amount, and, especially when campaigning, tend to repeat the same points multiple times daily while functioning on very little sleep and mostly bad food. Verbal miscues are only to be expected: and they are probably scrutinized more closely and judged more harshly in a politician like Bush—who, despite, or rather mainly because of, his elite educational background, chose to cultivate an anti- or at least non-intellectual persona—than in one like Barack Obama, who made no attempt to efface the signs of his own Columbia and Harvard education. Be that as it may, the arguable "unfairness" here only emphasizes how intent Stone and Brolin are in creating Bush as the protagonist of farce.

Yet the film's Bush is by no means *only* farcical. Just as Stone's Nixon, though certainly a villain, is not purely or one-dimensionally villainous in the way that viewers may have expected, so the buffoonery of Stone's Bush is only one aspect of his character. To focus exclusively on the kind of farcical moments discussed above could easily make the whole movie sound like an extended version of a skit on *Saturday Night Live* (NBC, 1975–present). But the film has much more to offer than that.

The perhaps surprising complexity of the film's central character seems, indeed, to have been one factor in its rather disappointing performance at the box office. Though *W.* made back its budget plus a modest profit, bigger things might reasonably have been expected of such an entertaining movie about a highly controversial president that was released while the latter was still in the White House. But the film appears to have fallen, commercially, between two stools. Bush's Gallup approval rating, which had soared to a stratospheric 90 percent shortly after the terrorist attacks of September 11, 2001, had sunk to a subterranean 25 percent when Stone's film hit the big screens in October 2008. That 25 percent was mainly composed of the fiercely loyal hard-core Republican base, whose members were not inclined to see their hero savaged (as they presumed) by a filmmaker of Stone's left-wing reputation.

Meanwhile, much of the disapproving or even, often, passionately Bush-hating majority (for Bush was more *personally* detested by his political opponents than any major Republican politician since Nixon himself) heard reports that the film's representation of their *bête noire* was not entirely unfavorable and was even, in some ways, surprisingly sympathetic: which did not put them in the mood to line up for tickets either. But the complexity of the central portrayal in *W.*—the way it achieves farce while also transcending it—helps to make it a film of enduring interest.

W.: The Man

Indeed, suggestions of something beyond farce can be found even in perhaps the most robustly farcical single scene: the 1966 Deke fraternity initiation mentioned above. As is customary in such ceremonies, a group of "pledges" (i.e., candidate members), Bush among them, are being abused in various verbal and physical ways by the full-fledged members of the frat. Stripped naked and made to kneel on the floor with their hands on top of their heads, the pledges are hit, loudly insulted, and sprayed with water; sometimes large amounts of hard liquor are literally poured down their throats with a funnel. (Years later, Bush will tell Cheney that the interrogation techniques being used by US forces on suspected terrorists remind him of his fraternity days.) There is also a more mental component to the initiation. One pledge is asked to give the names of the 40 or so frat brothers in the room. Uncertain and apparently somewhat terrified by the whole situation, he rattles off a few surnames, but his memory soon fails, and he is rewarded by the jeers of the brothers. Bush, contemptuously addressed as "Mr. Pussy," is called on next. Asked if he thinks he can do better, he says he thinks he can. Fluently and with no apparent hesitation, he then names one frat brother after another, not only identifying each by both first and last names, but also, in a foreshadowing of his habit as a politician, offering a usually alliterative (and evidently appropriate) nickname for every person he mentions: "Scotty 'Scotch and soda' Sonnenberg, Paul 'Putting-on-the-Rich' Richardson, Jackie 'Jambalaya' Jackson," and so forth. The room erupts in cheers, and one of the frat brothers running the initiation shouts with enthusiastic admiration, "We have got a working brain here! He may be from Texas, but he's gonna be one great Delta Kappster." Forced into a situation designed to make him as unimpressive as possible, W. has nonetheless managed to impress everyone. He is "Mr. Pussy" no longer.

To be sure, the scene is careful to make clear that Bush's triumph owes something to his family background. He is identified as a "legacy" pledge, his male ancestors stretching back to his great-great-grandfather all having been Dekes themselves (which must mean that his family has been involved with the fraternity for nearly all of its history, Delta Kappa Epsilon having been founded at Yale in 1844). It is also mentioned that Bush's grandfather, Prescott Bush, is currently one of Connecticut's own US senators (thus, in fact, misstating Senator Bush's tenure of office by a few years). Bush's success may also be partly due to his (that is, Josh Brolin's) striking good looks; at least, his handsome features and slim muscular build make a clear contrast with the appearance of the homely, overweight, bespectacled pledge who fails at the naming test just prior to his own triumph. Still, when all such allowances have been made—and whether Bush's performance is really extemporaneous, or whether, as is perhaps more likely, he has memorized the list of nicknames in advance, rightly calculating that it would probably come in handy sooner or later—the interpersonal skills that Bush has displayed are genuinely remarkable. To win over a room full of people who have gathered for the specific purpose of humiliating him and his fellow pledges (and who, as the film makes clear, mostly come from very wealthy families themselves) is a mark of the raw political talent that Rove will accurately detect many years later. More specifically, the ability not only to put a large number of names and faces together but also to remember (as the nicknames indicate) just enough about each individual to seem personally interested in each is an invaluable talent for an electoral politician (Lincoln was famous for it). Although only a fool, perhaps, would desire to become a Deke in the first place, the scene demonstrates that more than pure foolish buffoonery may be required to achieve this goal.

The film then cuts from the scene of the fraternity initiation to one of Bush's father (James Cromwell), now a US congressman, sitting at his desk and talking on the phone. As we soon figure out, he is speaking to a jailer in New Jersey, where W. (now Yale's head cheerleader) is locked up for leading some criminal vandalism in celebration of Yale's victory over Princeton in their annual football game. When he gets his son on the phone, Bush Senior at first seems almost sympathetic, reminiscing about his own Yale days and musing about how the only thing better than beating Princeton was beating Harvard. But he soon bears down on the younger Bush: "My father would have kicked the living crap out of me if I ended up where you are now, Junior." W. tries to minimize the seriousness of the situation, but the elder Bush will have none of it: "Now I'm getting you out of this, *this time*. I don't want to get any more phone calls like this again—ever."

In less than the first twelve minutes of running time, then, the film has offered three substantial scenes—of the war-planning conference at the White House, of the fraternity initiation, and of the conversation between father and son—that give ample scope to Bush as the buffoonish protagonist of farce while also, at the same time, indicating more complexity in its central character than *pure* farce could allow. Somewhat paradoxically, Bush is most impressive amidst the mere silliness of the Deke house. But he is not entirely unimpressive in the White House scene either. Though he may struggle to avoid confusing Iran and Iraq, he displays an effortless self-confidence in asserting mastery over a room full of people all of whom are more experienced and knowledgeable than he is. He knows the importance of mere physical posture in establishing dominance, and swaggers aggressively around the room as his subordinates remain literally beneath him, seated on sofas and chairs (except for Cheney, who slouches in a shadowy doorway, rather like a Dickensian villain). When Powell, who is clearly more than dubious about the wisdom of invading Iraq, suggests that containment would be the better policy, Bush rejects the notion with rhetoric specifically calculated to defeat the four-star military man: "That's a *defense*, General, not an offense." At the end of the meeting, Bush asserts what can only be called *spiritual* mastery over the group by insisting that they all join him in a moment of silent prayer: "You too, Turdblossom," he instructs Rove, who (like Cheney) does not seem quite comfortable communing with the Lord.

To be sure, we should not forget that the self-confident ability to impose one's will on others, which can be such a valuable political asset, owes much—again—to Bush's highly privileged background: the background that we will hear about in the fraternity scene that immediately follows the White House scene, and that we see at work in the scene that follows after that, as Congressman George Bush Senior promises to use his influence to insure that his son will face no serious consequences for his lawbreaking. Bush—like John Kennedy in this regard, and quite unlike Richard Nixon—cannot remember a time when he was not considered a very important person simply by virtue of being born into his family. The Bush family fortune may be more modest than the Kennedy centimillions, but their money is older, and the family has enjoyed political influence and high social position longer. (While W. could boast at the Deke house that his great-great-grandfather was a member of the fraternity at Yale, John Kennedy's great-great-grandfather seems to have been an impoverished peasant who lived and died in Ireland.)[68] Furthermore, as Episcopalians, the Bushes fit into the white Anglo-Saxon Protestant aristocracy of the American republic more smoothly and "naturally" than the Irish Catholic Kennedys. If ever there was a "fortunate son" in the sense conveyed by the Creedence Clearwater Revival song of that title, it was, as Stone's movie makes clear, George W. Bush.

But inherited advantages can carry one only so far (a point illustrated in actuality by the unimpressive careers of W.'s brothers, Neil and Marvin Bush—the former of whom, however, is completely absent from Stone's movie, while the latter makes only one brief appearance). Though Stone certainly does not suggest that George W. Bush was a political leader remotely comparable to John Kennedy in vision or creativity, *W.* does acknowledge that, for all that can be said about political "handlers" like Rove, nobody has ever gotten to the modern White House without abundant political talent of his own. Perhaps the most consequential exercise of political insight and ability that we see on Bush's part—achieved, as far as we can tell, without help from Rove or anyone else—occurs after his first, and failed, try for political office: his 1978 run for Congress against the conservative Texas Democrat Kent Hance (Paul Rae, looking a good deal more like a stereotypical Southern redneck than the real Hance ever did). In a scene showing a joint appearance by Bush and Hance in front of some Texas voters, Hance hammers away mercilessly at his opponent, denouncing Bush as an over-privileged Eastern "carpetbagger," with his inherited wealth and his Ivy League background. Hance brags that, in contrast to Bush's lineage, *his* father and grandfather were ordinary farmers, and that his own education was gained at public universities in Texas. Bush tries to point out that he has actually lived in Texas since the age of two, but Hance insists that W. remains an outsider "in good Christian country." Come election day, Bush does better than any other Republican has ever done in Texas's 19th district, but still loses to Hance; and, in politics, as Bush himself points out, "First is first, and second is nothing." But he resolves, "There's no way I will ever be out-Texaned or out-Christianed again." In a sense, Bush's entire future political career, which will contain nothing but electoral victories, is foreshadowed by that sentence. During the real-life Bush presidency, most Americans (and notably Bush's liberal opponents) seemed to assume, falsely, that the image of the president as an unsophisticated Texas good old boy represented his "natural" self rather than a persona shrewdly and deliberately constructed for political advantage.[69]

As with Stone's slightly cruel mockery of Bush's sometimes tangled English syntax, one might argue that the film, despite showing clear evidence of W.'s political ability, is nevertheless somewhat "unfair" in declining to display the full extent of the real-life Bush's talents. For instance, giving a set speech is a most important political function, and one at which Bush happened to excel. The speech that Bush gave to a joint session of Congress nine days after the al-Qaeda attacks of 9/11 surely ranks (whatever else may be said of it) as one of the most rhetorically effective performances of recent years by an American president in a time of national crisis. And the real-life Bush never seemed flustered by the fact that—as he must have at least vaguely known, even if his sense of the American past was as cloudy as Stone's film suggests—he was operating in direct historical competition with one of the most revered presidential addresses of all time, FDR's speech asking Congress for a declaration of war against Japan on the day after the attack at Pearl Harbor. *W.* does include some of this speech, but Brolin's delivery, while competent, is considerably less consummate than the real Bush's own (whereas, in *Nixon*, Anthony Hopkins's oratorical performances are always equal to or better than their historical counterparts). Still, even though the generic determinations of farce inhibit the degree to which Bush's talents can be portrayed (say, in comparison to an evenhanded historical documentary), the film, as we have seen, transcends farce sufficiently to make those talents evident.

But it is not *only* by genuine political ability that Stone's Bush becomes something more than a merely comical protagonist. *W.* is as concerned with its hero's private life as is *Nixon* (or, indeed, more concerned); and, as with the earlier film, family romance looms large. It is in this context that the film's W. seems worthy not just of a measure of technical respect for his political skills, but of something very much like personal sympathy. The parallel with *Nixon* is pertinent here, for no viewer of that film can be unmoved by the psychic violence that, as we discussed in the preceding chapter, was inflicted upon the young Richard by the savagely saintly Hannah Nixon; not to mention the lasting effects of that violence well into Richard's presidential adulthood. One difference, however, is that *W.* has no particular interest in the kind of mother-complex from which Stone's Nixon suffers. Barbara Bush (Ellen Burstyn) is a fairly prominent character, sometimes with a comical edge that to some degree parallels the more farcical elements in the representation of her son. In a sharp contrast to the persona of the restrained, dignified First Grandmother that the actual Barbara Bush managed to project in the mass media during the presidencies of her husband and her son, the Barbara Bush of the film is loud and vulgar in the peculiar way that only those completely secure in their upper-class status can be. But she is not portrayed as vitally important in the psychic formation of her eldest son (even though the general biographical understanding is that W., in real life, was raised mainly by his mother, Bush Senior having been taken away from home so often by his various political jobs). It is the *father*-son relationship that is crucial here. On one level, the film dramatizes an Oedipal battle as Freudian as one could ask for. While Stone and Burstyn's Barbara Bush is sometimes amusing, there is nothing the least bit funny about the film's President Bush Senior: especially if you happen to be his first son and namesake.

For "Poppy" Bush (as W. frequently calls his father) is consistently portrayed as the coldest and most demanding of Yankee patriarchs, repeatedly belittling his son for failing to live up to family expectations. In 1972, a few years after grudgingly getting Yale's head cheerleader out of a New Jersey jail, "Poppy" summons W. to his office to discuss the complete mess that his son has made of his post-college years: continual drinking to excess, failing (or just giving up) at a series of potentially lucrative career opportunities, and, to top things off, getting a girlfriend pregnant (at least according to the woman in question). "What are you cut out for?" asks Bush Senior, the icy calmness of his tone more devastating than any shouting or bluster could be. "Partying, chasing tail, driving drunk? What do you think you are—a Kennedy? You're a Bush. Act like one." The reference to the other major political family of modern America (though the Bushes at this point have yet to attain that status) is of course pointed; but what the scene most crucially illustrates is how Bush's background does not provide him *only* with advantages. It also comes with the psychic battering of always being told that he is failing to meet inherited standards. The privileged, fortunate son is also, in some ways, a most *un*fortunate son. The implicit comparison with the success that Bush Senior has made of his own life is doubtless painful enough. But what is probably worse for W., in this scene, is the *explicit* comparison with his own younger sibling: "Your brother Jeb graduates Phi Beta Kappa. What did you get? C's?" As we shall see, the patriarch's plain and stated preference for Jeb over W. will become a major motif of the film. Poppy promises to "take care" of the complaining girlfriend, but makes excruciatingly clear how disappointed and disgusted he is at having once again to clean up after W.

The following year, Bush achieves something that one might think would allow him—finally—to earn his father's respect. He gains admission to the Harvard Business School, the most prestigious academic institution of its type in the world. But things do not go well. W. decides to celebrate his acceptance by taking his underage brother Marvin (Keenan Harrison Brand) out for some drunk driving, and crashes the car upon returning home.[70] Poppy is furious: "I've had just about enough of your crap!" he tells his son. In earlier father-son confrontations, W. has tried to appear humble and respectful. But now, his aggressivity evidently fueled by whiskey, he pronounces himself as fed up with Poppy as Poppy is with him. He mockingly addresses his father as, "Mr.—what?—Perfect, Mr. War Hero, Mr. *God Almighty*!". The father-son struggle seems about to become an actual fistfight, until Jeb, at Barbara's urging, physically intervenes between the Oedipal combatants. When Barbara suggests to her husband that their son surely deserves some credit for getting into the highly selective business school, his reply is devastating: "Of course he got in! Who do you think pulled the strings?" W.'s psychic position is intolerable. He must endure his father's withering contempt even while depending upon him for everything, from getting out of jail to getting into Harvard. It is the perfect recipe for an agonizing identity crisis.

Even when asking W. for help, Poppy Bush manages to get in subtle or not-so-subtle digs, especially with regard to his preference for Jeb. He asks W. to come to Washington to assist with his 1988 campaign for the presidency: but goes a little out of his way to indicate that he had first asked Jeb, who proved to be unavailable. Though Bush does indeed seem to make a real contribution to his father's successful effort—largely by serving as his ambassador to the increasingly organized forces of the Christian Right, the political importance of which W. understands better than Bush Senior does—he senses, accurately, that he has nonetheless not really gained Poppy's esteem: "No matter what I do, it's just never gonna be enough," as he says to Laura. Even when actually trying to be nice to W., his father cannot help but communicate negative messages. In 1990, in the middle of his presidency, Bush Senior visits W. and congratulates him on the job he is doing as managing partner of a syndicate that owns a major-league baseball team. But he then muses on what a bright future he sees for *Jeb*, who, he says, could even become president someday. When W. decides to run for governor of Texas in 1994, both his parents strongly discourage him, with Barbara ridiculing his chance of winning. Bush Senior makes the real point: "This isn't fair to Jeb"—because he fears that W.'s campaign could somehow interfere with Jeb's own plans to get elected governor of Florida. When W. does indeed win his race, his father dutifully attends the inauguration but—as the newly elected governor clearly perceives—seems less happy for W. than depressed at Jeb's having lost in Florida.

Even being elected president of the United States cannot really repair Bush's relationship with his father. As the 2003 invasion of Iraq approaches, Bush Senior is deeply worried about its wisdom— rightly, of course, according to the political viewpoint of the movie— but declines to talk directly to his son. Instead, he tries to undermine him in a completely public way, by having Brent Scowcroft publish an essay in *The Wall Street Journal* arguing against the impending war. Scowcroft is not an on-screen character, but the film counts on the audience remembering him as not only an old personal friend of Bush Senior but also the latter's closest co-thinker on matters of foreign and military policy. When the essay appears, Condoleezza Rice is furious at Scowcroft (an old mentor of hers), but her boss knows who is really responsible: "He wouldn't be doing this unless my father approved it."

The film's final image of the father-son relation comes in a dream sequence as the debacle of the Iraq War has become obvious to all, and as W.'s approval rating has cratered. In the dream, President Bush walks into the Oval Office, only to find his father already there, sitting behind the presidential desk. Bush Senior points out that this used to be *his* office, taunts his son to fight *mano a mano*, and tells him (yet again) how deeply disappointed with his first-born he is. Poppy explains that W., with his war that has become "a goddamn fiasco," has ruined the once lustrous Bush name: "Two hundred years of work—for Jeb!"

The film shows Bush dealing with the intolerable pressure put upon him by his father in two not entirely unrelated ways: booze and Jesus. Alcohol is his constant crutch and companion from his teenage years until middle age, and getting drunk, apparently, is his favorite hobby (which is another reason he fits so well into his Yale fraternity). He is seldom without a beer in his hand, or, alternatively, a bottle of whiskey, or, failing that, anything else alcoholic, it seems, that happens to be available. Eventually, after waking up with an unusually nasty hangover the morning after celebrating his 40th birthday with Laura and some friends, he resolves to quit excessive drinking for good: and succeeds in doing so. But—though the screenplay does not use the actual term—the film suggests that the abstinent Bush is best understood as what specialists in the treatment of alcoholism call a "dry drunk": that is, an alcoholic who has managed to stop consuming alcohol, but without resolving any of the underlying psychological issues that led to the excessive consumption of booze in the first place. In this case, it is, of course, Bush's father-complex that remains the primary unresolved problem. One way the persistence of Bush's addictive personality is shown is by his continuing intense need for oral gratification: as manifest in his extreme loquaciousness and in the virtually compulsive way we see him consuming food and drink (as in the lunch scene with Cheney discussed above). Frequently, indeed, a bottle of beer remains his cherished companion, though the cameras are careful to show that the brand is O'Doul's, America's best-selling variety of "non-alcoholic" beer. But O'Doul's actually has an alcohol content of 0.4 percent—any beverage containing less than 0.5 percent alcohol is considered non-alcoholic by federal legal definition—and many experts discourage recovering alcoholics from consuming it.

Even more important than Bush's near-beer, iced tea, pecan pie, and other consumables is his religious conversion. He finds Christ at the same time that he gives up heavy drinking, and becomes an adherent of "born-again" Evangelical Christianity—primarily under the influence of the evangelist (and televangelist) Earle Hudd (Stacy Keach), the most important fictional character in the movie (though he is said to be partly based on a composite of various actual religious figures, including Billy Graham, who were important to the real-life Bush). The film's representation of Bush's religion is interestingly nuanced. Both Hudd and the born-again Bush are shown to be perfectly sincere in their faith, which does seem to play a genuinely supportive role in Bush's abstinence (or near-abstinence) from alcohol. At the same time, it also seems that, in moving from booze to Jesus, Bush has, at least to some degree, simply traded one addiction for another. There is, for instance, something compulsive and bullying in the way he is always forcing his religion into entirely secular situations. Just as he once took drunken joy in bringing his brother Marvin into the drinking life, so he later insists on the praying life even for those, like Rove, who would obviously prefer to stick to (secular political) business. But, at least, Jesus will not normally cause one to smash up a car. Most important here is the impact that W.'s conversion has on his relationship with his father. Bush Senior (though no teetotaler himself) has had utter contempt for his son's alcoholism, at one point vainly advising him to get himself to an Alcoholics Anonymous meeting. But, as we have seen, he has little choice but to accept the electorally vital help with the Christian Right that his son's religion and consequent religious connections make available to the 1988 campaign—even as Bush Senior maintains the personal distaste of an old-fashioned genteel Episcopalian for W.'s highly emotional version of Protestant Christianity.

The complexity of Stone's Bush is thus genuinely impressive. He is sometimes buffoonish, but he is also a politician of real talent, and, at the same time, he earns a good deal of the audience's sympathy not only for the continual psychic violence that he suffers in the paternal relation but also for his essentially unsuccessful ways of dealing with it. Though he is not a figure of high tragedy like Stone's Nixon, W. contains a good deal of tragedy's humbler (and much undertheorized) generic cousin, pathos. If often comical, W. is no less often pathetic. As such, he is a considerably more sympathetic character than his father (and Stone thus reverses, in a way, the dominant value judgment of the two real-life Presidents Bush assumed by most American liberals). Bush Senior is not only personally cold and withholding, but he seems to have no moral substance and no real principles beyond narcissistic family pride and a worship of worldly success. His preference for Jeb is clearly based on the fact that, of the Bush children, Jeb is the one that (as Barbara Bush at one point suggests) most closely resembles their father. W., by contrast, has a fearful moral sincerity about him—in his religious faith but also in his presidential policies. Toward the end of the film, as the Bush presidency has collapsed in disaster, a deeply depressed W. plaintively says to Laura in the privacy of their bedroom, "I mean, all I wanted to do is make this a better and safer world—for everyone." It is, of course, a darkly and unintentionally comical sentence when spoken by the man primarily responsible for the hideous mass slaughter in Iraq. Yet the sentence is also heartfelt and pathetic: It is easy to see why the film disappointed those who had hoped to see the ratification of such antiwar slogans as, "Bush lied, they died." Stone's Bush does not *think* that he lied. As we will see, the politics of W. exist in an unusually complex relation with perhaps the most searching portrayal of any individual personality in the Oliver Stone *oeuvre*, save only Richard Nixon.

W.: The War

Though W. is, as we have seen, a film more personally focused than *Nixon* and far more personally focused than *JFK*, it is, of course, like them, also a film about American political and military history. As with the earlier films, its primary political focus is on a war, with the Iraq War serving a thematic function very roughly equivalent to that served by the Vietnam War in the duology. Indeed, the temporal structure of *W.*, which is considerably simpler than that of either *JFK* or *Nixon*, itself emphasizes the centrality of the invasion of Iraq and its aftermath. The film proceeds on two parallel temporal tracks, and periodically switches from one to the other; the two tracks may be designated the *Bildungsroman* track and the war track. The former is primarily concerned with tracing the development of George W. Bush as an individual. Foregoing any treatment of childhood (and in this way distinguishing its method from that of *Nixon*), the *Bildungsroman* track begins in 1966 with the Deke initiation at Yale and concludes 33 years later, as Bush, now the recently re-elected governor of Texas, prepares to run for president in 2000. The entire presidential campaign of that year is elided, and so are the terrorist attacks of 9/11 and the launching of America's retaliatory war against Afghanistan. The war track begins in 2002 with the (almost) opening scene of Iraq War planning in the White House and continues through scenes of further war preparations, of the American invasion itself, and of the disastrous aftermath when "major combat operations" (Bush's own phrase) in Iraq have concluded. It may be tempting to consider the *Bildungsroman* track as constituting the more personal level of the movie, and the war track the more political level—and, to a certain degree, this is true. But the personal and the political are constantly overlapping with one another, and no dichotomy between them is possible. We should bear in mind that, if the two tracks were conflated, and the scenes re-arranged into chronological order, we would have a discontinuous but coherent history of Bush from successful fraternity pledge to failed president. In this history, the Iraq War is politically central.

In by far the best historical account of the politics of the real-life Bush family, Kevin Phillips (who, as it happens, was, during a much earlier phase of his career, one of the principal political strategists in Richard Nixon's 1968 campaign) outlines his thesis succinctly:

> In the United States . . . the twentieth-century rise of the Bush family was built on the five pillars of American global sway: the international reach of U.S. investment banking, the emerging giantism of the military-industrial complex, the ballooning of the CIA and kindred intelligence operations, the drive for U.S. control of global oil supplies, and a close alliance with Britain and the English-speaking community.[71]

Investment banking is pretty much absent from *W*.; Oliver Stone, the son of a stockbroker, has made two films about high finance—*Wall Street* (1987) and *Wall Street: Money Never Sleeps* (2010)—but otherwise has shown relatively little interest in the subject. For the rest, however, Stone's film—and in particular its focus on the Iraq War—squares quite well with Phillips's analysis. (Given Stone's penchant for exhaustive research, it seems a safe guess that he and his screenwriter Stanley Weiser had read Phillips's book, which came out four years prior to their film.) For example, though the movie does not delve into the complex associations with the CIA and US intelligence operations generally that were maintained by various of *W*.'s ancestors (George Bush Senior, at one point in his career, was CIA Director), it does show the centrality of intelligence to Iraq War planning. George Tenet is portrayed as having some reservations about some of the more fantastic intelligence sources sponsored by Cheney, but he is ultimately a loyal ally in making the invasion possible. Or again: The English-speaking alliance is nicely represented by a scene in which British Prime Minister Tony Blair (Ioan Gruffudd) pays a visit to *W*.'s ranch in Texas in order to discuss the coming Anglo-American assault on Iraq. Gruffudd's tones of voice, gestures, and facial expressions nicely convey what one imagines may well have been the real-life Blair's complexly mixed feelings, as he tries to pretend that he is a full-fledged partner in the coalition, even while it is repeatedly made evident to him that, though British assistance is welcome, all real decisions will be made exclusively by the Americans.

By far the most prominently represented, however, of Phillips's five "pillars" is the absolute determination that control of the world's oil supplies should remain forever in American hands. Bush himself seems more comfortable articulating less mercenary justifications for the invasion, from family resentment at the fact that President Saddam Hussein of Iraq once tried to have his father killed, to a deeply confused but on some level apparently sincere belief in democracy (and that Saddam maintained a cruel tyranny over his country can, after all, hardly be denied). But Bush allows his more forthright—and not at all buffoonish—vice-president to make the case that really matters. In a crucial war-planning scene at the exact midpoint of the film, various views are exchanged— for a while—as the president looks on mostly in silence. Cheney, supported by Rumsfeld, argues consistently for war. Powell argues against. Rice seems basically on the Cheney/Rumsfeld side, but hesitates to commit herself too clearly. Tenet stresses the menace of Saddam's arsenals as robustly as he can, but refuses to confirm that the Iraqi leader possesses nuclear weapons. Rove maintains that, without an invasion, the Bush Administration will probably not survive the 2004 election.

Finally, with the air of an adult who has allowed the children to play their games long enough, Cheney rises, walks toward a large electronic map, and proceeds to deliver a coldly brilliant illustrated lecture. In a quarter century, says the vice-president, America's own oil reserves will be gone; but the country's demand for oil will have increased by something like 30 or 40 percent. With only

5 percent of the world's population but consuming 25 percent of its energy, the United States will be separated by two oceans from the world's major oil reserves in Eurasia. What then? Iraq alone possesses a tenth of the world's oil, and 40 percent of all the oil that is extracted from the earth passes through the Strait of Hormuz. The only solution, as Cheney makes clear, is to maintain a permanent American military presence in the Middle East that will give the United States unchallengeable control over the production and distribution of the one commodity on which the country— and the world—depend absolutely. Furthermore, Cheney leaves little doubt that American dominance must be maintained over not only Iraq but also Iran, which sits atop the third-largest oil reserves on the planet. When Powell demands to know Cheney's "exit strategy" after the coming Iraq War, Cheney is quite frank in reply: "There is no exit. We stay." As he puts it a few moments later: "Control Iran, control Eurasia, control the world. Empire. *Real* empire. Nobody will fuck with us again." Bush is mightily impressed ("Big thoughts!" he exclaims), and it becomes evident that the unanimous sense of the room is now for war. The consensus includes, finally, even Powell—whose pro-war presentation to the United Nations will, as the film shows, be indispensable in paving the way for the invasion of Iraq. Bush proclaims it to have been "a great meeting—best yet," and brings it to a conclusion with (of course) a prayer.

As the film will make clear, there is nothing at all funny about the awesomely destructive Iraq War (as indeed, there was nothing funny about Louis Bonaparte's dictatorship). Yet Marx's terminology of tragedy and farce does have some pertinence to the contrast, both historically and in Stone's movies, between the Vietnam War— together with the larger Cold War of which it was the most sanguinary episode—and the Iraq War. The Cold War was massively destructive and wasteful, and (as John Kennedy pointed out) kept the world poised on the brink of the ultimate disaster of a global nuclear holocaust that would have destroyed not only all human civilization but virtually all the higher forms of life on the planet. Yet it had the grandeur of genuine ideological struggle. At least in their stated positions, both sides fought for real human values: the Soviet Union for peace and international solidarity; the United States for liberty and human rights. Since these values, however often violated in practice by *Realpolitik*, were not intrinsically or formally opposed to one another, one might argue that the Cold War actually contained, simply on the level of ideology, the potential for its own resolution. Such, indeed, is implicit in some of the deep rhetorical logic of Kennedy's 1963 commencement address at American University, which we examined in the first chapter of this volume. Though JFK's vision was cancelled in Dealey Plaza (as the first installment of Stone's duology has it), its nobility lives in the memory of Garrison and those like him, and also, in a strange and limited way, perhaps even in that moderating of the Cold War temporarily achieved by Nixon's foreign policy.

There is not a shred of even putative nobility in the rationale for the Iraq War outlined by the film's Cheney and by the film itself. The Vietnam War could inspire a sincere—but, of course, misguided and ultimately disillusioned—patriot like Ron Kovic (Tom Cruise) in Stone's *Born on the Fourth of July* (1989) to imagine, for a while, that, in volunteering to fight, he was upholding his country's finest values and traditions. The Iraq War, as Stone presents it, features no soldier even remotely comparable to Kovic. Cheney makes clear to the men (and one woman) making the Iraq War that it is being undertaken simply for the most cynical thievery and opportunism. The vice-president's own terminology makes explicit that this is classical imperialism pure and simple—and even with no real equivalent to "the white man's burden" or *la mission civilisatrice*, which had once served to give rhetorical and ideological reinforcement to the older imperialisms of Britain and France, respectively. Perhaps there was an element of tragedy in the Cold War. Though

JFK certainly gives full weight to the ultimately economic basis of the military-industrial complex (most notably in the tutorial that "X" gives to Garrison), it suggests that even those who organized the murder of the president may have also been motivated by sincerely ideological principles of Cold War anti-communism. Cheney makes clear that no such principles are involved in the Iraq War. Furthermore, the war does not, as it turns out, constitute the first easy step in the smooth takeover of Eurasian oil that the vice-president has outlined. Instead, and after a few deceptively straightforward US victories in pitched battles against Saddam's forces, the war soon degenerates into the most squalid imaginable farce, as American troops get bogged down in a seemingly endless nightmare of roadside bombs and improvised explosive devices. Unable to withstand the overwhelming superiority of American weapons in conventional combat, the Iraqis resist the invasion by means of guerilla warfare. The irony of the farce is almost unbearable: for (as Stone's Vietnam War trilogy has shown) it was, of course, guerrilla warfare that defeated the United States in Vietnam. There is again some sense of the world ludicrously turned upside down when the situation deteriorates so badly that the commander-in-chief is driven to demand of his top subordinates, "Who's in charge?" and "Why wasn't I told?".[72]

As in *Nixon*, Stone makes liberal use of archival nonfictional footage to show the enormous destruction of the Iraq War, displaying both the "shock and awe" of American air power and the much smaller but deadly ground counterattacks by the Iraqis.[73] Again as in *Nixon*, there is also significant file footage of antiwar demonstrations at home (and abroad), illustrating how Bush's war, like the war of Johnson and Nixon before him, tears at the civilian fabric of American society. But the war scenes of *W.* also contain something for which there is no precedent at all in *Nixon*: a scene of Bush, in company with Laura, and with no cameras to record the occasion for propaganda purposes, visiting wounded American troops in hospital. This scene, of all those in the film, portrays Bush at his most attractive and sympathetic. Though there are moments of *naïveté* that remind the viewer of W.'s buffoonish side—as when he suggests that an obviously poor Hispanic couple from Texas, the parents of a terribly wounded soldier, should pay a social call on his own parents when they get back to Houston—he is generally shown as both skilled and, so far as one can tell, perfectly sincere in comforting some of those who have been hideously maimed because they followed orders that were issued ultimately from his own desk. When a bedridden soldier says that he would like to stand up for the president, Bush replies, "No you don't, Sergeant. No, I'm the one standing up for you." Speaking with the Hispanic couple and their son, W. does his best to address them in Spanish— a language that the film represents him (in accord with most actual biographical reports) as having a serviceable though not completely fluent command.

Probably no scene in the movie was received less warmly than this one by those viewers who, in 2008, entered the theatre hoping to see their own utter detestation of George W. Bush ratified. Yet the scene's stress on Bush's sympathetic side, on his identity as something more than merely a buffoon, supplies an important clue to the film's ultimate insight, which in turn is what holds *W.* together as both a personal character study and a political meditation on American power. For it is precisely the element of sincerity and pathos in Stone's Bush that makes him so massively dangerous and destructive. Bush in the White House is, as he likes to say, the "decider." Why did he decide on the Iraq War? The Vietnam War as presented in *JFK* and *Nixon* sprang from the needs of the military-industrial complex and the geopolitical logic of the Cold War. Cheney, as we have seen, presents, in *W.*, the corresponding and wholly imperialist rationale for the Iraq War. But Cheney never had the power to order US forces into combat. Though Bush approves of Cheney's scheme, he is never presented as sufficiently devoted to what he himself calls "big thoughts" for such complex, long-term Machiavellianism plausibly to serve as his own primary motivation. Nor should we place much weight on the fact that Stone's Bush (like the real-life one) once expresses a personal grudge against Saddam Hussein because of the attempt on Bush Senior's life. Indeed, given the film's elaborate portrayal of the father-son relation, one might suspect that this could be one point on which W. actually feels a sneaking sympathy with Saddam—though doubtless at a level so profoundly repressed that he would never be able to admit the feeling even to himself.

Some weight *should* be placed on the fact that Bush likes to think of himself as a defender of democracy, as one who, as he says to Laura, desires a better and safer world for everyone. The proverb has it that the road to hell is paved with good intentions, and the film suggests that the hell Bush creates in the Middle East is to some degree the result of intentions that were not without moral sincerity (it is no accident that most of the film's final credits are accompanied by Bob Dylan's "With God On Our Side" on the soundtrack). Yet Bush's thinking on democratic institutions and related matters is so hopelessly muddled—we again recall the first scene of White House planning, in which the president, in a space of a few seconds, gratefully acknowledges and then completely forgets Condoleezza Rice's reminder that Iran holds democratic elections—that it is clear that much more must be involved in his decision to attack and invade a country that has never in any way threatened his own. What seems truly decisive here is Bush as the protagonist of pathos, as the perpetual loser of the Oedipal battle with his father. After a lifetime of psychic violence and subjugation at the hands of the paternal authority, Bush can find only one way to hit back decisively: not by the *mano a mano* fistfight he once drunkenly tried to initiate, but by toppling the same foreign despot whom Bush Senior left in power at the conclusion of the Gulf War in 1991. After his father has lost his re-election campaign against

Bill Clinton in 1992, W. attributes the defeat to Bush Senior being "weak in spirit," as evidenced, supposedly, by the failure to finish off Saddam. War is the key to W.'s assertion of strength, to his attempt finally to gain Oedipal superiority. "This is *my* war, not his," as he exclaims in anger at the publication of Scowcroft's antiwar essay, which, as W. plainly sees, has Bush Senior's fingerprints all over it. Yet, though he gets his war and gets rid of Saddam, the war turns into such a disastrous fiasco that Bush actually achieves nothing. The late dream scene in which W. is confronted by Bush Senior in the Oval Office shows that he realizes, at least in the unconscious realm of night, that the battle with his father remains forever lost. The fortunate son remains also unfortunate—but, of course, not nearly so unfortunate as the people of Iraq.

Finale

I will conclude this volume by briefly revisiting, in the light of the foregoing analyses of *JFK*, *Nixon*, and *W.*, some of the general theoretical issues first engaged in the Introduction. We may begin with a quite basic question: Why should one bother with historical fiction at all? There are, after all, whole libraries of nonfictional scholarship about the presidencies of John Kennedy and of Richard Nixon, and a considerable amount of scholarship even about the much more recent administration of George W. Bush. With such material available, why (the pleasures of entertainment aside) take the time to watch Oliver Stone's movies? Likewise, of course, there are ways to learn about the Jacobite rebellion of 1745 or the Napoleonic invasion of Russia that do not involve the fictionalizing performed by *Waverley* (1814) or *War and Peace* (1869)—just as one can read about the history of the civil wars and of the political maneuvering within the ruling class of fourteenth- and fifteenth-century England without attending performances of the history plays of Shakespeare.

Fundamental as this question may seem, it quickly resolves into one more fundamental yet: Why bother not just with historical fiction but with *fiction* at all? Why read novels, attend plays, or watch movies? For, as Georg Lukács was perhaps the first critic to see with full clarity,[74] historical fiction, in the sense exemplified by

179

the works referred to in the preceding paragraph, is less a special-
ized variety of fiction in general than something like the paradigm
of all fictional representation. Or, to put the matter another way, *all
fiction is in an important sense historical fiction.*[75] Of course, not
all of it deals with wars and obviously political struggles; not all of
it features the doings of kings and presidents and generals. But all
of it is based in one way or another on historical reality—there *is*
nothing else that it could possibly be based on—which, however,
it declines to represent in the apparently more straightforward
manner of nonfictional scholarship.

The very titles of the three films that this volume has focused
on announce their concern with public and indeed presidential
history. Similarly, we may consider a couple of sentences plucked
virtually at random from an early chapter of *Waverley*, which is
generally understood to have been the founding text of the historical novel in the narrow sense:

> A difference in political opinions had earlier separated the
> Baronet from his younger brother Richard Waverley, the father of
> our hero. Sir Everard had inherited from his sires the whole train
> of Tory or High-church predilections and prejudices, which had
> distinguished the house of Waverley since the Great Civil War.[76]

These words not only plainly allude to matters of obvious public
moment but even perform a historical move quite audaciously overt
by anchoring the novel's eighteenth-century narrative in the central
British cataclysm of the seventeenth century. Yet fundamentally
no less historical than *Waverley* is the almost exactly contemporary *Pride and Prejudice* (1813)—though the latter is often taken as
exemplifying fiction at the furthest remove from being historical in
the specific sense associated with Walter Scott and his successors
like Tolstoy. Consider its famous opening sentence: "It is a truth
universally acknowledged, that a single man in possession of a good

fortune, must be in want of a wife."[77] Despite its direct concern only with private domestic matters, the sentence conveys a good deal of the historical reality on which Jane Austen bases her fictionalizing. It indicates that the novel is set in a class society characterized by rampant economic inequality, and it suggests that heterosexual marriage can be important for the material fortunes of women. Of course, one need not read Austen's novels in order to learn about class and gender relations in Georgian England. Works of so-called "social history"—that is, the history of day-to-day life for ordinary people—are almost as easily available as works in the older and perhaps still somewhat better established tradition of political and military history. So, again: why bother with fiction?

The question of what kind of value fiction possesses—or whether, indeed, it possesses any serious intellectual value at all—is by no means a frivolous one. On the contrary, it is deeply rooted in the entire Western intellectual tradition. Near the very beginning of this tradition, we find, in the *Republic*, perhaps the most rigorous and sweeping attack on fiction ever offered. Plato would ban from his ideal commonwealth all poets—by which he means all practitioners of fiction, all who trade in figurative representations that are not strictly accurate *secundum litteram*. While the argument in all its detail is an intricate one, much of the case against poetry (which Plato also makes, though in a rather different way, in the *Ion*) essentially boils down to the charge that the poets do not really know what they are talking about: a claim that, as we have seen, many who are doubtless innocent of philosophic training have felt qualified to make far less elegantly than Plato about the films of the cinematic "poet" Oliver Stone, especially *JFK*. Though Plato's position has always been an extreme one, overtly embraced *in toto* by relatively few who have come after him, it has haunted nearly all Western thought about art and fictionality; and it has seldom been refuted quite as confidently and completely as the poets themselves—in the large sense—might wish. Hegel, for instance, valued art and fiction much more highly than Plato did, but considered them ultimately inferior to philosophy and destined to be superseded by it.

In an arena different from that of formal philosophy, the Platonic mistrust of fiction also retains considerable currency in what is called "the crisis of the humanities" in the academy today. Whether academic subjects like literature and drama and film should be adequately funded—or sometimes, indeed, whether they should even exist at all—is an increasingly open question in the pertinent discussions currently taking place. To many—including, on at least one notable occasion, President Barack Obama—it seems clear that such educational pursuits are less important, less worthy, and, perhaps above all, less *serious* than those devoted to the mastery of "harder" subjects like chemistry or engineering.

Often, to be sure, such judgments are expressed without any truly coherent theoretical justification at all, and merely on the stated basis of the most crudely philistine utilitarianism: It is widely believed (not quite accurately, as increasingly frantic academic humanists are often keen to point out) that the study of science and technology invariably brings economic benefits—both to the studying individual and to society at large—in a way that is not true of an education in the arts and humanities. Yet such ruthless bourgeois pragmatism is generally supported, even if at one or more removes, by a neo-Platonic suspicion that a knowledge of fiction is not actually knowledge *of* anything in particular: that it is, indeed, perhaps not really knowledge at all: and that it is certainly not knowledge in the sense offered by the physical sciences and their technological applications. (From this viewpoint, the so-called "social sciences," like economics or sociology or anthropology, are generally assumed to occupy an intermediate position, "harder" and more reliable than the arts and humanities though less hard than natural or "real" science.) What kind of knowledge—it is increasingly asked, overtly or implicitly—is gained by reading a story about people like Elizabeth Bennet and Fitzwilliam Darcy, who never actually existed? Or, to refer more specifically to the three Oliver Stone films discussed in this book: What is the point of a movie in which events and personalities taken incontestably from the historical record are shamelessly combined with frankly fictional and highly speculative elements?

One answer has been adumbrated in the Introduction to this book and may be developed a bit further here. The first, and arguably still the most effective, reply to Plato's attack on poetry and the mimetic arts generally was given by his former pupil Aristotle. As we have seen, Aristotle maintains that poetry, in the extended sense of imaginative mimetic fiction, is more "philosophical"—or, as we might put it, more intellectually rigorous and valuable—than the merely empirical or factual chronicle because it displays what *may* happen rather than simply what actually *has* happened. Poetry, that is, does not aim at the positivistic reproduction of contingent detail. Instead, it strives to disengage and display, out of the massive welter of (intrinsically pretty much meaningless) details presented by human reality, the fundamental patterns by which reality is shaped and by which it attains meaning. In other words, fiction, in the Aristotelian scheme *contra* Plato, does indeed provide not only genuine knowledge but knowledge of the most valuable sort: knowledge, that is, of the general and structural rather than the merely particular and accidental. Aristotle's counterargument against his old teacher has been enormously influential on most— or perhaps nearly all—of those who have tried to defend fiction against the Platonic dismissal that, however, has never, as we have seen, lost its own currency and force. The *Poetics* resonates in the thought, for example, of two such radically different modern neo-Aristotelians as T. S. Eliot and Georg Lukács. As noted in the Introduction, it stands behind Eliot's notion of the "essential history" that Shakespeare managed to "absorb"—and to represent in his plays—without recourse to the kind of innumerable specifics available in the British Museum. Equally, Aristotle's distinction between the merely factual chronicle and the truly poetic—and philosophical—representation is echoed in Lukács's crucial distinction between what he takes to be a lifeless naturalism that is bogged down in incoherently presented details, on the one hand, and, on the other, a genuine realism that rigorously grasps the major general dynamics of the historical process (see, for instance, the works by Lukács referenced above).

The analyses in the foregoing pages of *JFK*, *Nixon*, and *W.* should help to suggest some of the "essential history" displayed in the cinematic historical fictions of Oliver Stone. The most essential thesis in the essential history presented by these three films—which (to make the point again) are not exactly a trilogy but rather a duology plus an epilogue—is the political supremacy in modern America of the national-security state and the military-industrial complex. Ever since World War II (or, to put the matter in the terms maintained by the historical narrative of Stone and Kuznick in *The Untold History of the United States*, ever since Harry Truman rather than Henry Wallace succeeded to the presidency upon the death of Franklin Roosevelt), America, in the filmmaker's representation, has ceased to be a functioning democracy in any thoroughgoing sense. What above all has been "new in the American experience"—to employ the pregnant phrase from Dwight Eisenhower's Farewell Address that canonically named the military-industrial complex, and that Stone uses at the very beginning of *JFK*—has been the concentration of such enormous power at the top of the major repressive apparatuses of the national state as to raise the question of whether the nominally supreme civilian executive might be, as the unnamed Joanna Going character in *Nixon* puts it, relatively "powerless" in comparison. This is the central governing insight of all three films. It has been discussed earlier that a recurring character type in the Stone cinematic *oeuvre*, of which the Jim Garrison of *JFK* is a variant, is the ingenuous male protagonist who loses his innocence through a difficult and even shattering realization that the social norms he had been accustomed to take for granted—or even to embrace with enthusiasm—actually express, while concealing, vast evil. The type is surely an autobiographical one (and only most clearly and directly in *Platoon*). In filming the history of his country, Stone implicitly records his own personal history: the history of a man raised in a prosperous, conservative household, who attends an expensive Ivy League university and volunteers for combat in Vietnam, who as late as 1980 votes for Ronald Reagan for president, and who comparatively late in life comes to a lucid understanding of the structural danger and malevolence of the military-industrial complex against which Eisenhower warned.

The indeterminacy that structures so much of the epistemology of *JFK* also marks a dividing line between the Eliotic "essential history" recorded—or constructed—in the film, and the mass of contingent detail that, while certainly of interest, and while generically crucial for the melodramatic thriller, could be of *primary* importance only for the positivistic chronicle (in neo-Aristotelian terms) or the work of naturalistic fiction (in Lukácsian terms): forms that the cinematic text rejects in favor of what Lukács would call an authentic critical realism that grasps the fundamental currents of history.

Consider, for example, a question that, on some levels—certainly including the positivistic level of the criminal law—would be absolutely basic: Who shot Kennedy? The film melodramatically considers a vast number of particulars that could be relevant to this issue, but, as we have seen, is unable to supply any clear and confident answers. David Ferrie, according to (the fictional character) Willie O'Keefe, has been seen and heard advocating the murder of JFK and describing the "triangulation of crossfire" by which it could be accomplished. Was he, personally, one of the shooters? What about Lee Oswald, evidently an associate of Ferrie and O'Keefe, who, according to Garrison himself at one point, perhaps was ordered to take part in the assassination or perhaps was ordered to *prevent* it? Though the Warren Commission maintained that there was no doubt of Oswald's guilt as the lone gunman, was there ever really the kind of evidence that could have convicted Oswald in court, had he lived to stand trial? Senator Russell Long, in the conversation that first gets Garrison thinking seriously about the assassination, says that, were he investigating Kennedy's murder, he would round up a hundred of the world's most skilled riflemen and find out which of them was in Dallas on the fateful day. But how exactly could anyone, even with effective subpoena power, do that? Even if a group of marksmen that definitely included the shooters of Dealey Plaza could somehow be reliably identified— which itself seems impossible—would the shooters simply respond obediently to Long's hypothetical demands for information? On a grade presumably above that of the actual gunmen, Stone's film also encourages us to ask—but not to answer—the question of what role Clay Shaw played in the presidential assassination. Garrison and the film seem morally certain of the businessman's villainy, but the district attorney, as we see him personally prosecuting the case in court, does not even seriously attempt to present the kind of detailed factual evidence against Shaw that could possibly have led to a jury conviction.

Yet all such questions, however important in the courtroom, and however thrilling they may be in the melodramatic narrative, are strictly secondary to the essential history that it is the ultimate purpose of *JFK* to represent. What Garrison—and the viewer—come to understand is that the American power structure is crowned by a vast and permanent national-security establishment that is fabulously well-endowed financially and armed to the teeth. It is only to be expected that such a mighty complexus would fight against anything that it perceived to be a serious threat to its vital interests. All the lessons of history, as "X"—the Donald Sutherland character—maintains, point to that conclusion. If one assumes, as the film does, that Kennedy, in the final months of his life, did indeed intend such a threat—and there could hardly have been a greater such threat than the liquidation of the Cold War—then the *why* of the assassination becomes almost self-evident: and all else about the events of November 22, 1963, are just (largely uncertain) details. Indeed, even if, though perhaps most improbably, the national-security state did in fact *not* successfully conspire to murder its nominal commander-in-chief—and, after all, the only thing that the film offers as truly conclusive *proof* of conspiracy is the ballistic evidence that establishes the presence of at least two shooters over Dealey Plaza—that would only be a contingent oversight (or tardiness). It would change nothing fundamental that we know about the military-industrial complex. Kings are killed, as "X" says.

Nixon, of course, is a king who was not killed, save in the important psychological and symbolic sense that he was deprived of the presidency that he had twice won at the ballot box. The historical moments of Kennedy and of Nixon are the same: as is indicated not only by their direct contest against one another in 1960 but also by the fact that Nixon was born only four years before Kennedy and captured the White House only eight years after JFK did. Accordingly, almost exactly the same national-security apparatus is central to the essential history of *Nixon* as it is in *JFK*. Owing, however, to the sharp generic difference between the two films—between a thrilling melodrama with a huge cast of characters, on the one hand, and, on the other, a tragedy that centers insistently on a single protagonist—in *Nixon* the historical dynamic is, for the most part, refracted through the psychological exploration of the titular character. Of particular importance here, for example, is Nixon's paranoia: which, like some scholars who have attempted nonfictional psychological investigations into the thirty-seventh president,[78] Stone finds to be a salient category for understanding Nixon. Anthony Hopkins conveys the Nixonian paranoia in various effective nonverbal gestures, for instance the ways in which his eyes sometimes scurry around in nervous, frightened watchfulness, and in which his "body language" seldom suggests comfortable relaxation, especially in the presence of other people. But essentially the same message is also communicated more explicitly, perhaps most notably in several scenes of Dick and Pat Nixon *tête-à-tête* that have been discussed in some detail above. It will be recalled that Dick, pushing back against Pat's incredulity, insists that he really is beset with huge numbers of enemies, who care about nothing except destroying him personally (he says that, contrary to what the enemies claim, they do not even really care about the Vietnam War). He also maintains, in conversation with his wife, that he and only he is capable of fixing the deep trouble that America is in—megalomania being, as Freud says, as much a characteristic of paranoia as a persecution-complex.[79]

But, as the saying goes, even paranoiacs have enemies. Nixon's paranoia, in the Stone film, cannot be understood *only* as a psychological category or disorder. It also corresponds, in many respects, to the actual position that Nixon occupies *vis-à-vis* the military-industrial complex.[80] Most crucial here is the scene that is arguably the most significant in the entirety of the film, that between Nixon and Richard Helms in Helms's private office at CIA headquarters. The fear and nervousness that President Nixon displays in response to Helms's somewhat cryptic remarks about President Kennedy can indeed be taken as paranoid symptoms. But the film encourages us to believe that Nixon is quite *correct* in interpreting the CIA director to be suggesting that the national-security state, of which Helms is a high-ranking functionary—perhaps, indeed, by this point in time the most high-ranking of them all—dispatched Kennedy when he proved inconvenient to them and could do the same to Nixon if he shows insufficient fealty to the Cold War. (It will be recalled that the specific matter at issue is Helms's objections to Nixon's apparent willingness to accept the continuance of the

Castro government in Cuba.) Nixon, wiser (or just less courageous) than Kennedy in this regard, backs off. Though not without occasional qualms and doubts, he remains a loyal servant of the military-industrial complex that Kennedy, as Stone imagines, turned against in his final months. Nixon may not be exactly "powerless," as the nineteen-year-old woman played by Joanna Going somewhat hyperbolically puts it. But he understands the far greater power represented by intrinsically unimpressive men like Helms (and Hoover), and he knows that being in office—even in the Oval Office—is not necessarily the same thing as being in power: "[Y]ou don't fuck with Dick Helms—period." That may be a paranoid way to look at things, but it is also, as the film has it, a true one.

The Cold War is over, of course, by the time present of *W.* Indeed, the USSR itself has been gone from the map for ten years when George W. Bush assumes the presidency. Yet the national-security establishment whose official rationale was the "twilight struggle" against Soviet Communism (to borrow a phrase from JFK's Inaugural Address) remains, remarkably, as strong as ever: and, after the terrorist attacks of 9/11, the Bush Administration resolves to make it stronger yet. If the central lesson in essential history is provided most overtly, in *JFK*, by the tutorial that "X" gives to Garrison in Washington, and if the corresponding scene in *Nixon* is that of the private meeting between Nixon and Helms, then the equivalent in *W.* is the scene of Cheney's illustrated lecture, in which the president's own role is mostly that of an onlooker. As we have seen, the vice-president makes evident that the explicitly ideological struggle of the Cold War is now gone and, with it, whatever tragic grandeur may have attached to the American claims to be fighting for values like freedom and human rights—though such claims retain a vestigial, muddled presence inside W.'s own head. Now, as Cheney explains, the traditional instruments of classic imperialism—force and fraud—will be fairly naked in the projection of American power toward the goal of forever controlling the planet's oil reserves.

That such a reorientation of the military-industrial complex is not accomplished without some difficulty of adjustment at the CIA and the Pentagon—the paramount agencies of the national-security state—is perhaps implied by the reluctance initially displayed by George Tenet and, especially, Colin Powell. But both, like the organizations they represent, take up the imperialist project described by Cheney; and the Iraq War, the most violent enterprise undertaken by the military-industrial complex since the Vietnam War itself, devastates much of the Middle East.

In keeping with the large element of farce in the generic composition of *W.*, the president himself is represented as almost a bystander as the national-security state rolls on. Bush relates to the military-industrial complex with neither the principled (if late) opposition of JFK nor the wary, paranoically sensitive coexistence of Nixon: but rather with something more like satisfied indifference. Whether or not W. is to be seen as less intelligent than either of his twentieth-century predecessors, he certainly has less detailed interest than they in geopolitics, which never seems to engage his attention with the zest that, say, pecan pie does. This is perhaps the most convenient attitude from the standpoint of the national-security establishment itself. Nobody will ever need to threaten Bush as Helms threatens Nixon, still less to have him gunned down.

In addition to the neo-Aristotelian matter of "essential history" as represented on the screen (as on the stage or the page), there is, I will maintain, at least one other—though not unrelated—way that Stone's historical fictions, and fiction in general, may be defended against neo-Platonic mistrust. This approach derives from the theory of ideology pioneered by Louis Althusser and developed in the specific context of literary criticism by Pierre Macherey and Terry Eagleton.[81] Ideology, in this somewhat technical sense, does not refer (exclusively or even mainly) to a relatively coherent body of consciously held beliefs. Althusser's principal English translator defines ideology (with Althusser's approval) primarily as "the 'lived' relation between men and their world" (with "men" certainly to be understood here to mean men and women).[82] Ideology, that is, refers to the (largely unconscious) realm of everyday life. It refers to the way that the structural realities of essential history are actually *experienced*, on the ground as it were, by individual men and women in the course of the innumerable activities that comprise living day by day. To be sure, nonfictional scholarship has increasingly tried to attend to ideology in this sense, notably in the traditions of "social history" referred to above. But it is noteworthy that it has done so at least partly by employing techniques imported from fiction. For fiction seems to be uniquely well qualified to represent history as it is actually lived in personal and interpersonal relations. As Eagleton puts it,

> Literature, one might argue, is the most revealing mode of experiential access to ideology that we possess. It is in literature, above all, that we observe in a peculiarly complex, coherent, intensive and immediate fashion the workings of ideology in the textures of lived experience of class-societies. It is a mode of access more immediate than that of science [by which Eagleton, following Althusser, means primarily Marxist historical materialism, though also Freudian psychoanalysis], and more coherent than that normally available in daily living itself.[83]

What Eagleton says of literature can be applied to drama, cinema, and, indeed, all modes of aesthetic representation that do not strive primarily after empirical veracity *secundum litteram*.

It is noteworthy that, in Stone's presidential films, the representation of the ideologies of lived experience is focused mainly on the lives of those who exercise considerably more political power than most people do: most obviously, of course, the presidents themselves. In this, Stone distinguishes himself from many (though certainly not all) other left-wing artists and historians, who often prefer to focus on "history from below," on the experience of those who—whether by reason of class or race or gender or nationality or some other factor—are comparatively marginalized by the power centers of a given social formation. Yet one thing that these movies illustrate is the massive consequentiality of ruling-class politics as practiced, for instance, in the White House, surely the most prominent power center in the world. Perry Anderson, in defending the necessity of studying the formation and deformation of states, has pointed out "that secular struggle between classes is ultimately resolved at the *political*—not at the economic or cultural—level of society" (emphasis in original).[84] Correlatively, there is much of importance to be learned from the workings of ideology in the lives of those who sit at or near the top of political hierarchies, like presidents, or even those, like big-city district attorneys, who are much farther down the ladder but who nevertheless can exercise far more political impact than most of us can.

I will end this book by recalling just a couple of examples from the material discussed in the preceding pages. One of the clearest, perhaps, is the complex relation displayed in *W.* between the enormous death and destruction of the Iraq War and the Oedipal struggles of the titular character. In accord with most of the real-life testimony offered by those who have encountered George W. Bush personally—including some of his most unswerving political opponents, like the left-wing journalist Molly Ivins and, indeed, like Oliver Stone himself—the film portrays Bush as (in sharp contrast to his father) a fairly likeable human being on the interpersonal level. The scene in the military hospital is exemplary in this regard. Bush is by no means a villain in the sense known to melodrama, as Clay Shaw and Richard Helms are. Yet few villains of that sort have ever been responsible for as much suffering as Bush unleashed on the people of the Middle East. Psychically battered and bullied by his father for virtually his entire life—we see the process from W.'s college years onwards, but it presumably began much earlier than that—Bush has sought shelter from the paternal storm in beer and whiskey bottles, and in the arms of the Jesus known to Evangelical Protestantism. Finally, he finds what, briefly, *feels* like a truly adequate and satisfying counterattack in the Oedipal battle: He orders the US military into combat to overthrow the same Iraqi tyrant that Bush Senior left in place at the conclusion of his own war. Unfortunately, far more is destroyed than just Saddam Hussein, including W.'s own presidency.

On the structural level, of course, the American (or Anglo-American) invasion of Iraq—however botched and even counterproductive in the immediate term—is driven not by the president's psychic problems but by the global imperialist project outlined by the vice-president. One might even be tempted to say—as many observers actually did say during Bush's first term in the White House—that, in some ways, Dick Cheney seems to have been the real president. But the plain fact is that he was not. Cheney may have had a clearer and more articulate understanding than Bush of the needs of US capitalism and the military-industrial complex; but he never commanded a single soldier. Outside of what Bush chose to grant him, Cheney had no power at all beyond those powers granted by the US Constitution (to break tie votes in the Senate and to succeed to the White House upon the death or removal from office of the president). To some degree, the relation in *W.* between vice-president and president resembles, or expresses, or gestures toward what we have discussed earlier as the delicate balance that Stone maintains between deterministic and heroic perspectives on history, between Tolstoy and Carlyle, between the structural and the personal levels. The large forces that drive the capitalist national-security state are always more powerful than any individual, Bush included. But that does not mean that individual choices, and the lived ideologies that drive *them*, count for nothing. Doubtless *something* of the sort that Cheney describes in his illustrated lecture would, sooner or later, have found concrete political and military expression—even if W. and Bush Senior had enjoyed the most untroubled and harmonious father-son relationship in the world. But it would not, presumably, have been exactly the war that both the film and real history actually know—and, possibly, it would not have been anything quite as deadly.

Finally, let us turn to a key element in *Nixon*, surely the aesthetically finest of the three presidential films. We have seen how, in the movie, Nixon's personal struggle against the Kennedys—and more generally against the "elite," of which they are, for him, the purest and most compelling representatives—is, among other things, a kind of petty-bourgeois class struggle. Marx and Engels describe the petty bourgeoisie as a *transitional* class: Its members possess capital, but so little of it that, in competition with members of the big or "real" bourgeoisie, they are constantly being threatened with financial ruin and thus with being forced downwards into the ranks of the wage-earning proletariat.[85] The petty bourgeois enjoys bourgeois status, but does so marginally and, above all, very *insecurely*. Individuals of petty-bourgeois origin may, of course, respond to their situation by choosing to join forces with the proletariat and to embrace the cause of socialism. But, historically, that has not been the most common or prominent pattern. The more typically petty-bourgeois attitude has been to cling, desperately and frantically, to whatever shards of bourgeois status that the petty bourgeois manages to hang onto: and, often, to support not socialism or even liberalism, but the most reactionary political movements, which characteristically promise to fulfill the petty bourgeois's deepest desires for middle-class respectability. The petty bourgeois is in this way ideologically stuck between classes, fearing and despising the working class—the dreaded *terminus ad quem* of enforced proletarianization—while envying and resenting those able to feel serenely unassailable in their bourgeois identity.

As Stone's film makes abundantly clear, Nixon was not only a petty bourgeois but a petty bourgeois of the most completely classical sort. He was born into a family of small shopkeepers, and Stone's cameras go rather out of the way to show us the shabby wooden grocery store (*cum* gas station) that provided the Nixons' livelihood during Richard's childhood and youth. The divided and even contradictory set of political attitudes to which this background of lived experience might be expected to give rise does, indeed, accurately describe President Nixon's stance with regard to the military-industrial complex and the US power establishment in general. He remains their faithful servant, but is never really tranquil or satisfied in this role. Even beyond resenting John Kennedy's Harvard education and the practically endless supply of money with which Joseph Kennedy Sr. was able to support his son's political career, Nixon harbors more general grudges against "the CIA, the Mafia, those Wall Street bastards," and the American ruling class as a whole. As we have seen, he is even capable of once suggesting to J. Edgar Hoover, of all people, that the antiwar demonstrators who have come to Washington to protest against his own prosecution of the Vietnam War may perhaps have a point after all. As an *echt* petty bourgeois, Nixon will uphold the interests of the ruling class and the national-security state. But he will never love them or feel at home among their top functionaries.

It is in this light that we can return yet one more time to the scene of Nixon's private meeting with Richard Helms, the most powerful person with whom we ever see him interacting. It may be—it is not, admittedly, an idea explicitly suggested in either *JFK* or *Nixon*, but it is certainly one that we are permitted to entertain as a possibility—that it was precisely the fact that John Kennedy was born into what Nixon calls "the elite" that made him feel sufficiently invulnerable that he was able (as Helms reminds us, and as "X" has reminded us in *JFK*) to threaten to smash the CIA. In any case, events, as Stone constructs them in the duology, showed that even the power of the Kennedy centimillions combined with that of the White House was to prove no match for that of the nation's truly supreme rulers.

Nixon, by contrast, combines petty-bourgeois dissatisfaction and resentful truculence with ultimate petty-bourgeois timidity. He makes the trip to Helms's office in Virginia ostensibly to read him the riot act and to issue certain orders, and at first attempts to do exactly those things. But he soon backs down. By the end of the meeting, Nixon has given Helms everything Helms wants—most importantly guarantees of increased funding for the CIA and of Helms's own re-appointment as the agency's director—and has received hardly anything in return save for vague promises. But then—and especially since, as we have seen, *JFK* always hovers in the backstory of *Nixon*—we are surely meant to conclude that, in a point, perhaps, for petty-bourgeois ideology, it is Nixon's obeisance to the national-security state that saves his life.

Notes

1. A notable exception on this last point is *Alexander* (2004), which does, however, implicitly suggest parallels between the conquests of Alexander the Great and US foreign policy during the Iraq War.

2. My analysis of the two Wall Street films may be found in "Character and Capital in the Wall Street Films of Oliver Stone," *Film International* 14, no. 3–4 (2016): 43–54.

3. Jan Kott, *Shakespeare Our Contemporary*, trans. Boleslaw Taborski (London: Methuen, 1967), 3–167.

4. T. S. Eliot, "Tradition and the Individual Talent," in *The Sacred Wood* (London: Methuen, 1920), 52.

5. *Aristotle's Theory of Poetry and Fine Art*, trans. S. H. Butcher (New York: Dover, 1951), 35.

6. In fact, one Richard was *almost* named after the other. Richard Nixon's mother was fascinated by English history and named all but one of her sons after various English kings. Richard, however, was named after Richard I, Richard Cœur de Lion, not after Richard of Gloucester.

7. Carl Freedman, *The Age of Nixon: A Study in Cultural Power* (Winchester: Zero Books, 2012).

8. My references to the film in what follows are based on the director's cut as available on the DVD released by Warner Home Video in 1997 and on the Blu-ray released by Warner Home Video in 2008. The director's cut is slightly longer than the original theatrical release (206 minutes, as against the latter's 189) and contains a few extra scenes. However,

nearly everything in the film that I quote or to which I specifically allude can be found in the theatrical release (which has not been available in the United States on home physical media since a VHS tape released in 1992, which I have also consulted).

9. Tom Wicker, "Does *JFK* Conspire Against Reason?," in *JFK: The Book of the Film*, ed. Oliver Stone and Zachary Sklar (Montclair: Applause, 1992), 246. This volume contains an annotated version of the screenplay but also a great many journalistic responses to the film, the vast majority of them strongly unfavorable. A further reference to Wicker's article will be given parenthetically by page number.

10. As late as 1980, Stone voted for Reagan. He moved politically leftward comparatively late in life. See Matt Zoller Seitz, *The Oliver Stone Experience* (New York: Abrams, 2016), 274.

11. The column was published in *The Washington Post* and is most readily accessible at https://www.washingtonpost.com/archive/opinions/1991/12/26/jfk-paranoid-history/1353d5cd-9d26-4088-acf7-d3ba5a0f8a0d/?utm_term=.3cfc498f1a30.

12. See Seitz, *The Oliver Stone Experience*, 465, n.9.

13. Ebert's review can be accessed at https://www.rogerebert.com/reviews/jfk-1991.

14. Ebert's Great Movie essay on *JFK* can be accessed at https://www.rogerebert.com/reviews/great-movie-jfk-1991.

15. I will consistently refer to the man alleged by the Warren Commission to be Kennedy's assassin as "Lee Oswald," the name by which he was universally known throughout his life. Though his middle name was indeed Harvey, he never went by all three names. The widespread habit of referring to him as "Lee Harvey Oswald" seems to have two sources. First, the public initially heard of him through police reports, and the Dallas police followed the standard procedure of referring to him by the full name that they had recorded. Second, the name of Lincoln's assassin, John Wilkes Booth, was very much a household term in 1963—far more so than it is today—and appears to have insinuated a subtle connection between presidential assassins and three names. Almost certainly on a

mostly unconscious level, calling the man "Lee Harvey Oswald" made him *seem* more like the man who shot the president.

16. A few of the more prominent examples are Edward Jay Epstein, *Inquest: The Warren Commission and The Establishment of Truth* (New York: Viking, 1966); Mark Lane, *Rush to Judgment: A Critique of the Warren Commission's Inquiry into the Murders of President John F. Kennedy, Officer J. D. Tippit, and Lee Harvey Oswald* (London: Bodley Head, 1966); Harold Weisberg, *Whitewash: The Report on the Warren Report* (Hyattstown, MD, 1966); L. Fletcher Prouty, *JFK: The CIA, Vietnam, and the Plot to Assassinate John F. Kennedy* (New York: Carol Group, 1992); Jim Garrison, *On the Trail of the Assassins: My Investigation and Prosecution of the Murder of President Kennedy* (New York: Sheridan Square, 1988). The last two texts named were especially important for the making of Stone's *JFK*.

17. The historian Michael Kurtz—whose own view of the accuracy of the history presented in *JFK* combines sympathy with astringent criticism—judges, "With the exception of *Uncle Tom's Cabin*, Harriet Beecher Stowe's explosive novel dramatizing the horrors of the institution of slavery, *JFK* probably had a greater direct impact on public opinion than any other work of art in American history" (Michael Kurtz, "Stone, *JFK*, and History," in *Oliver Stone's USA: Film, History, and Controversy*, ed. Robert Brent Toplin [Lawrence: University Press of Kansas, 2000], 174). There are other works that might be mentioned in this regard: Edward Bellamy's utopian novel *Looking Backward* (1888), which almost overnight called into being a mass movement devoted to Bellamy's version of socialism, one that found institutional form in more than 150 "Bellamy Clubs" in the United States alone; Upton Sinclair's naturalistic novel *The Jungle* (1906), which led to important action by the US government to provide for the (relative) purity of the American food supply; and D. W. Griffith's film *The Birth of a Nation* (1915), which helped to inspire the rebirth of the Ku Klux Klan and gave an enormous boost to white supremacy generally. Still, Kurtz's judgment is not implausible.

18. David Cecil, *The Young Melbourne: And the Story of His Marriage With Caroline Lamb* (London: Constable, 1939), 15. Further references will be given parenthetically by page number.

19. Indeed, Byron might well be described as the *first* literary celebrity in anything like the modern sense.

20. There is a story that, when president-elect, Kennedy asked Mrs. Roosevelt what he could do to get her, and the liberals in general, to think better of him. She gave him a simple answer: "Make Adlai Secretary of State." He didn't, of course. See David Halberstam, *The Best and the Brightest* (New York: Random House, 1972), 22.

21. Irving Howe, "The Fate of the Union: Kennedy and After," *The New York Review of Books*, December 26, 1963; most easily accessible at https://www.nybooks.com/articles/1963/12/26/the-fate-of-the-union-kennedy-and-after-5/. An earlier document of particular interest here is Norman Mailer's essay, "Superman Comes to the Supermarket," originally published in *Esquire* shortly before the 1960 election. It went on to become the single most famous thing that has ever been written about JFK, as well as one of the founding documents of the "New Journalism" of the 1960s and 1970s. As the title (which is not ironic) implies, the tone of the piece is strongly pro-Kennedy, so much so that Jackie Kennedy was moved to send Mailer a thank-you note in response; and Mailer himself later admitted that he wrote the essay with the intention of helping JFK to get elected. Yet Mailer's enthusiasm was entirely for Kennedy's *style*, not his policies. Even while virtually in love with the presidential candidate, Mailer could see Kennedy's essential political conservatism. Here is his comparison of Kennedy and Nixon: "Yes, America was at last engaging the fate of its myth, its consciousness about to be accelerated or cruelly depressed in its choice between two young men in their forties who, *no matter how close, dull, or indifferent their stated politics might be*, were radical poles apart, for one was sober, the apotheosis of opportunistic lead, all radium spent, the other handsome as a prince in the unstated aristocracy of the American dream" (emphasis added). The essay is best consulted today in the profusely illustrated hardback edition edited by Nina Wiener and published by Taschen (Cologne, Germany, 2014); the quotation is from pp. 79–80.

The book contains perhaps the finest collection of Kennedy photographs ever assembled in a single volume.

22. When Kennedy heard that the elder King had been opposing his candidacy on religious grounds, he is said to have commented to Harris Wofford, his chief adviser on matters of civil rights, "That was a hell of an intolerant statement, wasn't it? Imagine Martin Luther King having a father like that." Then he added: "Well, we all have our fathers, don't we?" Joseph Kennedy was widely known as a racist and anti-Semite, though his attitudes seemed to have softened when it became clear to him that blacks and Jews were among his son's strongest supporters. See Ted Sorensen, *Kennedy* (New York: Harper, 2009), 33. The volume was originally published in 1965.

23. See Richard Reeves, *President Kennedy: Profile of Power* (New York: Simon & Schuster, 1993), 61–62.

24. Or, as Howe, "The Fate of the Union," put it in December 1963: "[O]n the crucial issue of civil rights, he lagged at first, responded only after a great mass movement of Negroes exerted heavy pressure, and then failed to understand that there are some issues on which it is better, both morally and politically, to go down fighting than to back away shrewdly."

25. See Reeves, *President Kennedy*, 125.

26. References to *Rashomon* are to the digital restoration produced by the Criterion Collection in 2008.

27. See Seitz, *The Oliver Stone Experience*, 257.

28. All references to *Citizen Kane* are based on the two-disc special edition put out by Warner Home Video in 2001.

29. A remarkable stabilized editing of the Zapruder film is available at https://www.youtube.com/watch?v=Sqk3sdfXFkc.

30. To be strictly accurate, there are a few moments in Stone's movie which replicate portions of the Zapruder film and in which Kennedy is impersonated by the actor Steve Reed.

31. See John Hersey, "Survival," *The New Yorker*, June 17, 1944; most easily accessible at https://www.newyorker.com/magazine/1944/06/17/survival-2.

32. Given the film's overall view of its titular hero, it is unsurprising that the Inaugural Address—and therefore, in particular, the connection between the Address's pledge to "pay any price," etc. and the Vietnam War—is completely elided in *JFK*. Interestingly, though, two years earlier Stone, in an early scene of *Born on the Fourth of July*, had made this exact connection quite clear—perhaps almost too painfully clear.

33. See Garry Wills, *The Kennedy Imprisonment: A Meditation on Power* (Boston: Little, Brown, 1982), 269.

34. A clue to Khrushchev's own opinion on the matter may be that, according to one report, the Soviet leader told the legendary American diplomat Averell Harriman that he considered Kennedy's AU speech to be the finest given by any American president since Franklin Roosevelt. See James W. Douglass, *JFK and the Unspeakable: Why He Died and Why It Matters* (Marynoll, NY: Orbis Books, 2008), 45–46.

35. Perhaps the most lucid and persuasive scholarly argument in support of precisely this conclusion is to be found, unsurprisingly, in Oliver Stone and Peter Kuznick, *The Untold History of the United States* (New York: Gallery Books, 2012), 294–323. One might further argue that Kennedy, though generally fairly conservative and conventional, was on occasion capable of strikingly unconventional thought: so that his putative turn against the Cold War would not have been entirely out of character. One example of Kennedy's sometime independence of mind is his speech on the floor of the Senate in 1957 in which he attacked French colonialism in Algeria and the Eisenhower Administration's tacit support of the French. This speech, which caused great jubilation in Algeria (and the Afro-Arab world generally) and great consternation in Paris and in the US State Department, was extraordinary for an American public official—though it is true that Kennedy's anti-imperialism was largely based on his conviction that the ability of the United States to compete with the Soviets in the Third World would be seriously hampered if it was seen to be supporting old-style European colonialism. Another example occurred also in 1957, in a more casual setting. On a television interview program, the interviewer noted

that Senator Kennedy's wife was expecting a baby soon, and asked the senator whether he would want the child—if a son—to follow his own footsteps into public service. JFK replied that yes, he would want that, *whether the child was a son or a daughter*—and directly challenged the interviewer's premise by adding that he did not think political life should be reserved only for men. Almost *nobody*, certainly nobody among prominent political figures, talked like that in the America of the 1950s. (In the event, of course, the child was a daughter, and the footage of the 1957 interview was widely replayed in 2009, when Caroline Kennedy Schlossberg was prominently mentioned as a possible candidate for the US Senate seat that Hillary Clinton vacated to become Barack Obama's secretary of state. She did not become a senator but did serve for four years as Obama's ambassador to Japan.)

36. The sentence is usually attributed to the author and environmentalist Edward Abbey, though Garrison, in the film, refers to him only as "an American naturalist."

37. See Garrison, *On the Trail of the Assassins*, referred to above.

38. The most thorough scholarly biography of Garrison is the two-volume work by Joan Mellen: *A Farewell to Justice: Jim Garrison, JFK's Assassination, and the Case That Should Have Changed History* (Dulles, VA: Potomac, 2005), and *Jim Garrison: His Life and Times, the Early Years* (Southlake, TX: JFK Lancer, 2008).

39. Quoted in Monica Crowley, *Nixon Off the Record* (New York: Random House, 1996), 29.

40. See Stephen E. Ambrose, *Nixon: The Education of a Politician 1913–1962* (New York: Simon & Schuster, 1987), 210–11. The money—the equivalent of over $10,000 in current terms—of course came from Kennedy's father, Joseph Kennedy Sr.

41. Quoted in Crowley, *Nixon Off the Record*, 30.

42. Quoted in Ambrose, *Nixon*, 434.

43. See John F. Kennedy, *Profiles in Courage*, Memorial Edition (New York: Harper and Row, 1964), especially chapters 6 and 7.

44. In 1960, Nixon and Kennedy were, or seemed, sufficiently similar that Arthur Schlesinger Jr. felt moved to publish a short book entitled

Kennedy or Nixon—Does it Make Any Difference? (New York: Macmillan, 1960). As the court historian of the Kennedy family, Schlesinger naturally argued that it made a great deal of difference indeed.

45. For a far more detailed account of Nixon's career, see Freedman, *The Age of Nixon*, especially chapter 1. The 1960 contest between Nixon and Kennedy is most extensively dealt with in chapter 5.

46. T. S. Eliot, "Wilkie Collins and Dickens," in *Selected Essays*, Third Enlarged Edition (London: Faber and Faber, 1951), 467–469. A further reference to this essay will be given parenthetically.

47. I am indebted to one of the anonymous peer-reviewers for Intellect who reminded me that, in recent years, there has been a good deal of critical work on melodrama that continues its "rehabilitation" as an aesthetic form that is advocated in Eliot's essay. The pertinent work is extensive, but a particularly good example is Linda Williams's use of the category of melodrama in order to understand David Simon's all but universally praised television series, *The Wire* (HBO, 2002–2008). See Linda Williams, *On "The Wire"* (Durham, NC: Duke University Press, 2014), 1–7 and 79–136.

48. *Aristotle's Theory of Poetry and Fine Art*, trans. S. H. Butcher (New York: Dover, 1951), 45. A further reference will be given parenthetically.

49. *The Greek Plays*, ed. Mary Lefkowitz and James Romm (New York: Modern Library, 2017), 322. The translation is by Frank Nisetich.

50. The reference is to the 2018 film of *King Lear* produced by the BBC and Amazon Studios and directed by Richard Eyre—in which Anthony Hopkins's performance as Lear is at several points directly reminiscent of his performance as Nixon nearly a quarter of a century earlier.

51. See, among many other sources, Ambrose, *Nixon*, 36; Jonathan Aitken, *Nixon: A Life* (Washington, DC: Regnery, 1993), 14–15; Roger Morris, *Richard Milhous Nixon: The Rise of an American Politician* (New York: Henry Holt, 1990), 50ff.

52. Perhaps the most succinct statement of this principle occurs in Freud's 1905 book *Three Essays on the Theory of Sexuality*, one of the two or three

most foundational works of psychoanalysis: "A sadist is always at the same time a masochist" (quoted from the James Strachey translation [New York: Basic Books, 1975], 25). The most notable counterargument against Freud on this point is Gilles Deleuze's long essay, "Coldness and Cruelty," which argues for a sharp distinction between sadism and masochism. See Gilles Deleuze and Leopold von Sacher-Masoch, *Masochism*, trans. Jean McNeil (New York: Zone Books, 1991), 7–138.

53. Few biographies have contributed more to our knowledge of the thirty-seventh president than Anthony Summers, *The Arrogance of Power: The Secret World of Richard Nixon* (New York: Viking, 2000), to which we owe our understanding of Nixon's extensive and skillfully hidden financial corruption. Summers also recounts that Nixon was in the occasional habit of physically attacking his wife—a claim that (unlike Summers's other claims) was hotly denied by the Nixon family when the book was first published. Since the volume appeared five years after Stone's film, it is of course possible that Stone was unaware of Summers's research—though also conceivable that he could have had advance knowledge of Summers's findings. In any case, the Nixon created by Stone and Hopkins seems very unlike a batterer.

54. The real-life Nixon came to agree with this interpretation of things. In the summer of 1977, he took part in a series of interviews with the British television personality David Frost. One of Nixon's most remembered comments from the Frost interviews—notable for its expressly sadomasochistic language—was "I gave them a sword, and they stuck it in, and they twisted it with relish. I guess, if I'd been in their position, I'd have done the same thing."

55. We should remember that Mao's statement that Nixon came from a poor family is false, though it is a falsehood that the real-life Nixon himself frequently promulgated. As we have seen, Nixon's background was modest and lower-middle-class. His family was certainly far from rich (the way—interestingly—so many of his political opponents were: not only the Kennedys but also Adlai Stevenson, Nelson Rockefeller, and others), but the future president never knew genuine poverty of the sort

that so many Americans experienced in the 1930s. Perhaps, in the film, Mao is assumed to be aware of all this but is accepting Nixon's frequent self-characterization as a way of somewhat softening the harsh diagnosis he is making.

56. Mao's phrase is of course vague, and raises the question of just how many Vietnamese were actually killed in their war of self-defense against the Americans. The number will never be known with real precision, but one plausible estimate comes from a source unlikely to be suspected of anti-American bias: Robert McNamara, the US secretary of defense during most of Lyndon Johnson's presidency, who, aside from Johnson himself, was more responsible than any other single individual for the escalation and Americanization of the war that followed the JFK assassination. Many years after the war, McNamara estimated that 3.8 million Vietnamese had died in it. Of course, not all those deaths took place during Nixon's time in the White House; but most probably did. See Stone and Kuznick, *The Untold History of the United States*, 387.

57. On at least one occasion, *Nixon* makes what appears to be a quite specific allusion to *Death of a Salesman*. Near the end of the film, during his last evening in the White House, Nixon, alone with Kissinger, says, "You're the only friend I got, Henry." The line is striking because nothing in the movie—nor, for that matter, in the historical record—has suggested that Nixon and Kissinger were intimate or cordial personal friends, however closely they worked together professionally. But the line echoes something that Willy Loman, as he approaches his own catastrophe, says to his brother-in-law: "Charley, you're the only friend I got. Isn't that an amazing thing?" (*The Portable Arthur Miller*, ed. Christopher Bigsby [New York: Penguin, 1995], 95).

58. For a detailed discussion of Nixon and the press in real history, see *The Age of Nixon*, 198–212.

59. The subtitle of the single most penetrating study ever written of the historical Nixon (though marred by some errors that may have been almost unavoidable at the time) is significant: Garry Wills, *Nixon*

Agonistes: The Crisis of the Self-Made Man (New York: New American Library, 1970).

60. Thomas Carlyle, *On Heroes, Hero-Worship, and the Heroic in History*, ed. David R. Sorensen and Brent E. Kinser (New Haven: Yale University Press, 2013), 21 and 41, respectively. The volume was originally published in 1841.

61. The denial may be found in an interview with Helms, available on the official CIA website: see https://www.cia.gov/library/center-for-the-study-of-intelligence/kent-csi/vol44no4/pdf/v44i4a07p.pdf, p. 8.

62. The situation with the extant versions of *Nixon* is somewhat more complicated than that with *JFK*. Whereas the differences between the theatrical release and the director's cut of the earlier film are relatively minor, the director's cut of *Nixon* is so superior to the theatrical version that it would be difficult (or impossible) to gain a truly adequate understanding of the film from the latter. The most important difference is the inexplicable deletion from the theatrical release of the structurally and thematically essential scene in Richard Helms's office; Stone himself has expressed regret for the deletion (quoted in Seitz, *The Oliver Stone Experience*, 329). My references to *Nixon* in this chapter are accordingly based on the director's cut as available on the "Election Year Edition" DVD released by Cinergi Pictures and Buena Vista Home Entertainment in 2008 and on the Blu-ray released by the same companies in the same year. I have, however, also consulted the theatrical version as available on the undated DVD and the undated VHS tape released by the same companies; the tape (though not, oddly, the DVD) does contain the Helms scene as a "special feature."

63. Karl Marx, *The Eighteenth Brumaire of Louis Bonaparte*, trans. Ben Fowkes, in Karl Marx, *Survey from Exile: Political Writings Volume II*, ed. David Fernbach (New York: Random House, 1973), 146.

64. All quotations to and references to the movie are based on the Lionsgate DVD released in 2008.

65. Lyndon B. Johnson styled himself as LBJ for exactly the same reason. It is noteworthy that, as memories of Roosevelt have faded and the

country has generally drifted rightward on economic issues, no subsequent president, not even any of the three Democrats (Carter, Clinton, and Obama), has chosen to be known by three initials.

66. The fact that the United States has had two presidents of the same surname chronologically separated by only eight years has, for obvious reasons, been a source of confusion. In what follows, "Bush" will refer to George W. Bush, the forty-third president, while his father, the forty-first president, will be known as "Bush Senior" or some other unambiguous designation.

67. See, for instance, Stone's documentaries *Comandante* (2003), *South of the Border* (2009), *Castro in Winter* (2012), and *Mi Amigo Hugo* (2014).

68. And John Kennedy represented only the *second* generation of his family to attend Harvard. It is perhaps worth mentioning that Oliver Stone attended Yale (for one year) at the same time as Bush and, like him, was a "legacy" Yalie, Stone's father having also attended. Bush and Stone apparently never met while in New Haven. See this 2018 interview with Stone in *Business Insider*: https://www.businessinsider.com/oliver-stone-bush-biopic-w-militarization-more-dangerous-than-trump-2018-10.

69. "He [George W. Bush] is as disciplined a candidate as we have ever watched" (Molly Ivins and Lou Dubose, *Shrub: The Short But Happy Political Life of George W. Bush* [New York: Random House, 2000], 49). This is arguably the most intelligent biography of W. yet produced, written by life-long students of Texas politics.

70. One might suppose that this incident represents the screenplay at its maximum of creative freedom from the historical record. In fact, however, it seems to be biographically accurate. See Ivins and Dubose, *Shrub*, 13.

71. Kevin Phillips, *American Dynasty: Aristocracy, Fortune, and the Politics of Deceit in the House of Bush* (New York: Viking, 2004), 2.

72. In a section of his book, titled "Texas Macho and the Vietnam-Iraq Continuum" (*American Dynasty*, 293–301), Phillips interestingly argues that the political culture of Texas was the source of some continuity between the Vietnam War and the Iraq War. This is, however, not a

matter much emphasized in Stone's films, though it is not ignored completely.

73. "Shock and awe" was named and theorized in a 1996 study by the military intellectuals Harlan Ullman and James Wade. They described the strategy as "utterly brutal and ruthless," and intended "to achieve a level of national shock akin to the effect that dropping nuclear weapons on Hiroshima and Nagasaki had on the Japanese." They opined that shock and awe "can easily fall outside the cultural heritage and values of the U.S." Quoted in Stone and Kuznick, *The Untold History of the United States*, 525.

74. Three of Lukács's most important works in this regard are *The Historical Novel* (1937), *Studies in European Realism* (1950), and *The Meaning of Contemporary Realism* (1955).

75. In a discussion related to this one, I have analyzed the relation between historical fiction and science fiction in Carl Freedman, *Critical Theory and Science Fiction* (Hanover, NH: Wesleyan University Press, 2000), 44–62.

76. Sir Walter Scott, *Waverley* (London: Everyman, 1969), 66.

77. *The Oxford Illustrated Jane Austen*, ed. R. W. Chapman, Volume Two, Third Edition (Oxford: Oxford University Press, 1932), 3.

78. See Vamik D. Volkan, Norman Itzkowitz, and Andrew W. Dod, *Richard Nixon: A Psychobiography* (New York: Columbia University Press, 1997), for instance, 128–39.

79. See the Schreber case-history—"Psychoanalytic Notes Upon an Autobiographical Account of a Case of Paranoia (Dementia Paranoides)"—in Sigmund Freud, *Three Case Histories*, ed. Philip Rieff (New York: Collier, 1963), notably 167 ff. The case-history was originally published in 1911.

80. I have long been interested in the ways that paranoia can be considered "true," especially in the context of the conspiratorial national-security state: See Carl Freedman, "Late Modernity and Paranoia: The Science Fiction of Philip K. Dick," in Carl Freedman, *The Incomplete Projects: Marxism, Modernity, and the Politics of Culture* (Middletown, CT: Wesleyan University Press, 2002), 147–60. An earlier version of the

essay was published originally in *Science-Fiction Studies* (March 1984), 15–24, and that version has been reprinted several times.

81. The key texts here are Louis Althusser, "Ideology and Ideological State Apparatuses (Notes toward an Investigation)" (1969); Louis Althusser, "Freud and Lacan" (1969); Pierre Macherey, *A Theory of Literary Production* (1966); and Terry Eagleton, *Criticism and Ideology: A Study in Marxist Literary Theory* (1976).

82. See Louis Althusser, *For Marx*, trans. Ben Brewster (London: NLB, 1977), 252.

83. Terry Eagleton, *Criticism and Ideology: A Study in Marxist Literary Theory* (London: NLB, 1976), 101.

84. Perry Anderson, *Lineages of the Absolutist State* (London: Verso, 1979), 11.

85. See Karl Marx and Friedrich Engels, *The Communist Manifesto* (New York: Monthly Review Press, 1968), 15–20. The text was originally published in 1848.

Bibliography

Aitken, Jonathan. *Nixon: A Life*. Washington, DC: Regnery, 1993.

Althusser, Louis. *For Marx*. Translated by Ben Brewster. London: NLB, 1977.

———. "Freud and Lacan." In *Lenin and Philosophy and Other Essays*, 195–219. Translated by Ben Brewster. New York: Monthly Review, 1971.

———. "Ideology and Ideological State Apparatuses (Notes toward an Investigation)." In *Lenin and Philosophy and Other Essays*, 127–86. Translated by Ben Brewster. New York: Monthly Review, 1971.

Ambrose, Stephen. *Nixon: The Education of a Politician 1913–1962*. New York: Simon & Schuster, 1987.

Anderson, Perry. *Lineages of the Absolutist State*. London: Verso, 1979.

Aristotle. *Aristotle's Theory of Poetry and Fine Art*. Translated by S. H. Butcher. New York: Dover, 1951.

Austen, Jane. *The Oxford Illustrated Jane Austen*. Edited by R. W. Chapman. Volume Two. Third Edition. Oxford: Oxford University Press, 1932.

Carlyle, Thomas. *On Heroes, Hero-Worship, and the Heroic in History*. Edited by David R. Sorensen and Brent E. Kinser. New Haven: Yale University Press, 2013.

Cecil, David. *The Young Melbourne: And the Story of His Marriage With Caroline Lamb*. London: Constable, 1939.

Crowley, Monica. *Nixon Off the Record*. New York: Random House, 1996.

Deleuze, Gilles. "Coldness and Cruelty." In *Masochism*, 7–138. By Gilles Deleuze and Leopold von Sacher-Masoch. Translated by Jean McNeil. New York: Zone Books, 1991.

Douglass, James W. *JFK and the Unspeakable: Why He Died and Why It Matters*. Marynoll, NY: Orbis Books, 2008.

Eagleton, Terry. *Criticism and Ideology: A Study in Marxist Literary Theory*. London: NLB, 1976.

Ebert, Roger. "*JFK*." https://www.rogerebert.com/reviews/jfk-1991.

———. "Great Movie: *JFK*." https://www.rogerebert.com/reviews/great-movie-jfk-1991.

Eliot, T. S. "Tradition and the Individual Talent." In *The Sacred Wood*, 47–59. London: Methuen, 1920.

———. "Wilkie Collins and Dickens." In *Selected Essays*, 460–70. Third Enlarged Edition. London: Faber and Faber, 1951.

Epstein, Edward Jay. *Inquest: The Warren Commission and the Establishment of Truth*. New York: Viking, 1966.

Freedman, Carl. *The Age of Nixon: A Study in Cultural Power*. Winchester: Zero Books, 2012.

———. "Character and Capital in the Wall Street Films of Oliver Stone." *Film International* 14, no. 3–4 (2016): 43–54.

———. *Critical Theory and Science Fiction*. Hanover, NH: Wesleyan University Press, 2000.

———. "Late Modernity and Paranoia: The Science Fiction of Philip K. Dick." In *The Incomplete Projects: Marxism, Modernity, and the Politics of Culture*, 147–60. Middletown, CT: Wesleyan University Press, 2002.

Freud, Sigmund. "Psychoanalytic Notes Upon an Autobiographical Account of a Case of Paranoia (Dementia Paranoides)." In *Three Case Histories*, edited by Philip Rieff, 103–86. New York: Collier, 1963.

———. *Three Essays on the Theory of Sexuality*. Translated by James Strachey. New York: Basic Books, 1975.

Garrison, Jim. *On the Trail of the Assassins: My Investigation and Prosecution of the Murder of President Kennedy*. New York: Sheridan Square, 1988.

Halberstam, David. *The Best and the Brightest*. New York: Random House, 1972.

Helms, Richard. "An Interview with Richard Helms." https://www.cia.gov/library/center-for-the-study-of-intelligence/kent-csi/vol44no4/pdf/v44i4a07p.pdf.

Hersey, John. "Survival." *The New Yorker*, June 17, 1944. https://www.newyorker.com/magazine/1944/06/17/survival-2.

Howe, Irving. "The Fate of the Union: Kennedy and After." *The New York Review of Books*, December 26, 1963. https://www.nybooks.com/articles/1963/12/26/the-fate-of-the-union-kennedy-and-after-5/.

Ivins, Molly, and Lou Dubose. *Shrub: The Short But Happy Political Life of George W. Bush*. New York: Random House, 2000.

Kennedy, John F. *Profiles in Courage*. Memorial Edition. New York: Harper and Row, 1964.

Kott, Jan. *Shakespeare Our Contemporary*. Translated by Boleslaw Taborski. London: Methuen, 1967.

Kurosawa, Akira. *Rashomon*. DVD. Criterion Collection, 2008.

Kurtz, Michael. "Stone, *JFK*, and History." In *Oliver Stone's USA: Film, History, and Controversy*, edited by Robert Brent Toplin, 166–77. Lawrence, KS: University Press of Kansas, 2000.

Lane, Mark. *Rush to Judgment: A Critique of the Warren Commission's Inquiry into the Murders of President John F. Kennedy, Officer J. D. Tippit, and Lee Harvey Oswald*. London: Bodley Head, 1966.

Lefkowitz, Mary, and James Romm, eds. *The Greek Plays*. New York: Modern Library, 2017.

Lukács, Georg. *The Historical Novel*. Translated by Hannah and Stanley Mitchell. Lincoln, NE: University of Nebraska Press, 1983.

———. *The Meaning of Contemporary Realism*. Translated by John and Necke Mander. London: Merlin, 1963.

———. *Studies in European Realism*. New York: Grosset & Dunlap, 1964.

Macherey, Pierre. *A Theory of Literary Production*. Translated by Geoffrey Wall. London: Routledge & Kegan Paul, 1978.

Mailer, Norman. *Superman Comes to the Supermarket*. Edited by Nina Wiener. Cologne: Taschen, 2014.

Marx, Karl. *The Eighteenth Brumaire of Louis Bonaparte*. Translated by Ben Fowkes. In *Surveys from Exile: Political Writings Volume II*, edited by David Fernbach, 143–249. New York: Random House, 1973.

Marx, Karl, and Friedrich Engels. *The Communist Manifesto*. New York: Monthly Review Press, 1968.

Mellen, Joan. *A Farewell to Justice: Jim Garrison, JFK's Assassination, and the Case That Should Have Changed History*. Dulles, VA: Potomac, 2005.

———. *Jim Garrison: His Life and Times, the Early Years*. Southlake, TX: JFK Lancer, 2008.

Miller, Arthur. *The Portable Arthur Miller*. Edited by Christopher Bigsby. New York: Penguin, 1995.

Morris, Roger. *Richard Milhous Nixon: The Rise of an American Politician*. New York: Henry Holt, 1990.

Phillips, Kevin. *American Dynasty: Aristocracy, Fortune, and the Politics of Deceit in the House of Bush*. New York: Viking, 2004.

Prouty, Fletcher L. *JFK: The CIA, Vietnam, and the Plot to Assassinate John F. Kennedy*. New York: Carol Group, 1992.

Reeves, Richard. *President Kennedy: Profile of Power*. New York: Simon & Schuster, 1993.

Schlesinger, Arthur (Jr.). *Kennedy or Nixon—Does It Make Any Difference?*. New York: Macmillan, 1960.

Scott, Walter. *Waverley*. London: Everyman, 1969.

Seitz, Matt Zoller. *The Oliver Stone Experience*. New York: Abrams, 2016.

Sorensen, Ted. *Kennedy*. New York: Harper, 2009.

Stone, Oliver. *JFK*. DVD. Warner Home Video, 1997.

———. *JFK*. Blu-ray. Warner Home Video, 2008.

———. *Nixon*. DVD. Election Year Edition. Cinergi Pictures and Buena Vista Home Entertainment, 2008.

———. *Nixon*. Blu-ray. Election Year Edition. Cinergi Pictures and Buena Vista Home Entertainment, 2008.

———. "Oliver Stone says comparing 'disaster' of Bush's presidency to Trump is ridiculous and 'trivializes the situation,' as he reflects on his biopic *W.* 10 years later." *Business Insider*, October 29, 2018. https://www.businessinsider.com/oliver-stone-bush-biopic-w-militarization-more-dangerous-than-trump-2018-10.

———. *W.* DVD. Lionsgate, 2008.

Stone, Oliver, and Peter Kuznick. *The Untold History of the United States*. New York: Gallery Books, 2012.

Summers, Anthony. *The Arrogance of Power: The Secret World of Richard Nixon*. New York: Viking, 2000.

Volkan, Vamik D., Norman Itzkowitz, and Andrew W. Dod. *Richard Nixon: A Psychobiography*. New York: Columbia University Press, 1997.

Weisberg, Harold. *Whitewash: The Report on the Warren Report*. Hyattstown, MD, 1966.

Welles, Orson. *Citizen Kane*. DVD. Warner Home Video, 2001.

Wicker, Tom. "Does *JFK* Conspire Against Reason?". In *JFK: The Book of the Film*. By Oliver Stone and Zachary Sklar. Montclair, NJ: Applause, 1992.

Will, George. "*JFK*: Paranoid History." *The Washington Post*, December 26, 1991. https://www.washingtonpost.com/archive/opinions/1991/12/26/jfk-paranoid-history/1353d5cd-9d26-4088-acf7-d3ba5a0f8a0d/?utm_term=.3cfc498f1a30.

Williams, Linda. *On "The Wire"*. Durham, NC: Duke University Press, 2014.

Wills, Garry. *The Kennedy Imprisonment: A Meditation on Power*. Boston: Little, Brown, 1982.

———. *Nixon Agonistes: The Crisis of the Self-Made Man*. New York: New American Library, 1970.

Zapruder, Abraham. "The Zapruder Film." https://www.youtube.com/watch?v=Sqk3sdfXFkc.

Index

As there is considerable overlap between film characters and historical figures, a completely unambiguous separation within the index has not been possible. Therefore, to avoid duplication of entries, individuals have been indexed as if the film character and the real person are the same—unless there is a clear distinction on the page (e.g. Anthony Hopkins and Richard Nixon).

Sub-heads referring to "Bush" indicate George W. Bush; George Bush Sr. appears as Bush Sr.